Contents

3 The Format   22

4 The Production   29

5 Assessment   40

All about the National Curriculum

CHRIS EMERSON
IVOR GODDARD

HEINEMANN
EDUCATIONAL

Heinemann Educational, a division of
Heinemann Educational Books Ltd,
Halley Court, Jordan Hill, Oxford OX2 8EJ

OXFORD   LONDON   EDINBURGH
MELBOURNE   SYDNEY   AUCKLAND
SINGAPORE   MADRID   IBADAN
NAIROBI   GABORONE   HARARE
KINGSTON   PORSTMOUTH NH (USA)

First published 1989

ISBN 0 435 80616 5

Produced by AMR

201011

6 Reporting the Results

7 The Timing of the Introduction — Primary (Key Stages 1 and 2)

---

8 The Timing of the Introduction – Secondary (Key Stages 3 and 4)

9 Implications for Schools   77

10 In-Service Training and Other Support   86

Preface

The aim of this book is to draw together in a readily accessible form the basic information which has been published to date about the National Curriculum. It draws on Government documents and circulars, the reports of Working Groups established by the Government and documentation from the National Curriculum Council and the School Examinations and Assessment Council. The authors wish to acknowledge their debt to these sources.

It is not possible to write about the National Curriculum without considering its implications for LEAs, schools, teachers, parents and pupils. However, the authors have attempted to avoid, as far as possible, giving their own personal views or interpreting the documentation in other than a completely neutral way. Where conclusions are drawn or predictions made, it is in the knowledge that much of the detail of the implementation of the National Curriculum has yet to be determined and that these tentative conclusions may well require adjustment in the light of events.

This book has been written by two authors who between them bring a background of teaching, advisory work, INSET, examining, assessment and educational administration and who are now actively involved in discussing and planning the implementation of the National Curriculum.

1 The Background

The post-war era

The post-war years 1945-1975 were times of fundamental educational change. Underpinned by the Education Act 1944 the system developed to create the right for all children to greater access to free education. Over these years nursery education expanded to cater for an increasing number of under-fives. The move to comprehensive education in the secondary sector and the consequent abolition of selection at 11+ brought alterations in practice in both primary and secondary schools. The raising of the compulsory school leaving age to 16 gave all pupils a statutory right to eleven years of education. There was a massive expansion in higher education opportunities following the publication of the Robbins Report and the creation of several new universities.

Within schools there were revolutions in the curriculum and in teaching and learning styles. The application of active learning methods to an integrated curriculum within the primary schools made those schools exemplars of good educational practice far beyond Great Britain. In the secondary sphere, curriculum development such as that innovated by the Nuffield Projects in the sciences, the School Mathematics Project, the Schools Council History Project and the Geography for the Young School Leaver (GYSL) movement eventually influenced mainstream practice in all these subjects. Much seminal work on the curriculum was also sponsored and fostered by the Schools Council for the Curriculum and Examinations.

During this period there had also been changes in assessment. The introduction of GCE Advanced and Ordinary Levels in the early 1950s was followed by CSE in the 1960s so that a national examination was available for a large proportion of the ability range at 16. Already by 1970 the existence of two forms of examination at 16 was seen as unsatisfactory and the first moves were being made to bring together GCE O level and CSE into one system of examination.

Yet all these changes were carried out largely within and by the education establishment. The Secretary of State for Education and Science was of course seen as being in overall control of the system but that control was delegated, certainly as far as the delivery of the curriculum was concerned. The Secretary of State was responsible for the broad thrust of policy and the provision of resources. The curriculum was still a secret garden into which only educationalists were permitted entry.

The Ruskin College speech and the Great Debate

It was during the premiership of James Callaghan that this situation started to change. Mr Callaghan devoted a speech at Ruskin College, Oxford in October 1976 to educational matters, a speech which initiated the so-called Great Debate. He identified a number of concerns which have been returned to increasingly by politicians during the subsequent years:

- **Higher standards** '. . . higher standards than in the past are required in the general educational field. It is not enough to say that standards in this field or that have not declined. With the increasing complexity of modern life we cannot be satisfied with maintaining existing standards let alone observe any decline. We must aim for something better.'
- **Core Curriculum** 'It is not my intention to become enmeshed in such problems as whether there should be a basic curriculum with universal standards – although I am inclined to think that there should be . . . The goals of our education, from nursery school through to adult education, are clear enough. It is to equip children to the best of their ability for a lively, constructive place in society and also to fit them to do a job of work. Not one or the other, but both . . . Both of the basic purposes of education require the same essential tools. These are basic literacy, basic numeracy, the understanding of how to live and work together, respect for others, respect for the individual.'
- **Meeting the needs of industry** 'But I am concerned . . . to find complaints from industry that new recruits from the schools

sometimes do not have the basic tools to do the job that is required . . . There seems to be a need for a more technological bias in science teaching that will lead towards practical applications in industry rather than towards academic studies.'

■ **Influence of non-educationalists** 'I repeat that parents, teachers, learned and professional bodies, representatives of higher education and both sides of industry, together with the Government, all have an important part to play in formulating and expressing the purpose of education and the standards that we need.'

Thus was the Great Debate initiated, one form of which was a series of conferences around the country to which participants from a wide spectrum of interests were invited. Although there were no immediate tangible outcomes from this debate, many seeds had been sown which were to germinate and bear fruit over the succeeding years.

The Conservative Government and Sir Keith Joseph

The General Election of May 1979 saw the return of a Conservative Government and the introduction of an economic policy directed towards reducing inflation and increasing the efficiency of British industry. The following years brought widespread unemployment which eventually peaked at a figure of over 3 million; unemployment amongst the young was particularly severe. It was during this time that the Government began to express the idea that unemployment was caused partly through the lack of basic skills in the work-force. Unemployment was the fault not of the Government but of the unemployed themselves − and by implication the educational system which had failed to equip young people with the appropriate knowledge and skills. Thus Government attention was directed increasingly to the education service.

The appointment of Sir Keith Joseph as Secretary of State for Education and Science in 1981 brought to the post a man who was prepared to immerse himself in all aspects of the education system. He was concerned that education should be appropriate for students of all abilities − he felt in particular that the system was failing many pupils of average and below average ability. He believed that more precise definitions of desired levels of attainment would provide explicit goals which would give both teachers and students concrete targets at which to aim. This process of concentrating attention on what had to be achieved would in itself, he thought, raise standards of teaching and learning.

In January 1984, in addressing the North of England Conference in Sheffield, he set a long-term aim of raising pupil performance at all levels of ability so as to bring 80-90 per cent of all 16 year old pupils at least to the level of attainment presently achieved by pupils of average ability in individual subjects; and to do so over a broad range of knowledge, understanding and skills in a number of subjects.

GCSE and TVEI

Sir Keith used GCSE to begin the process of definition and articulation which is now being carried through in greater detail at all points in the primary and secondary curriculum. He agreed to the introduction of GCSE only on condition that National Criteria were drawn up which would form the framework of this new examination and would lay down the core of knowledge, understanding and competencies to be contained in syllabuses in the most popular subjects. External ground rules for syllabuses were established and for the first time, Examination Boards ceded their absolute right to approve and examine any syllabus they wished.

Sir Keith also asked that grade criteria should be evolved in each subject so that it was clear what a candidate awarded a particular grade in that subject had achieved. The Examining Groups are still wrestling with the technical difficulties inherent in such a system but again Sir Keith's aim of criterion referenced targets are reflected in the National Curriculum.

The education world was also shaken when in 1983 the Government established the Technical and Vocational Education Initiative (TVEI). Organised not by the Department of Education and Science but by the Manpower Services Commission under the Department of Employment, TVEI pilot schemes were established in a number of LEAs. TVEI courses were aimed at the 14-18 age range, boys and girls equally over the whole ability range, and were to be designed to provide a broad general education with a strong technical element. The initiative is now generally accepted as having influenced in a major way the design and delivery of the whole secondary curriculum. The initiative was eventually to be taken up on a pilot basis by most LEAs, and in an extension phase it is now intended that it should be spread in due course to all secondary schools in the maintained sector.

'Better Schools'

In March 1985 the White Paper *Better Schools* was published. The first two paragraphs set the context of the next part of the debate which was to result in the introduction of the National Curriculum:

'The quality of school education concerns everyone. What is achieved by those who provide it, and by the pupils for whom it is provided, has lasting effects on the prosperity and well-being of each individual citizen and of the whole nation . . . The Government's principal aims for all sectors of education are first, to raise standards at all levels of ability; and second, since education is an investment in the nation's future, to secure the best possible return from the resources which are found for it . . . There is much to admire in our schools; many of them cope well, and some very well, with their increasingly exacting task. But the high standards achieved in some schools throw into relief the shortcomings, some of them serious, of the others. Nor are the objectives which even the best schools set themselves always well matched with the demands of the modern world.'

The White Paper then established a general objective and explained the Government's own responsibility:

'By the time they leave school, pupils need to have acquired, far more than at present, the qualities and skills required for work in a technological age. Education at school should promote enterprise and adaptability in order to increase young people's chances of finding employment or creating it for themselves and others . . . The Government has a duty to take a lead in securing improvement . . . The duty of the Government is to ensure as far as it can that, through the efforts of all who are involved with our schools, the education of the pupils serves their own and the country's needs and provides a fair return to those who pay for it.'

Deficiencies in the Education Service

The White Paper proceeded to identify certain deficiencies in the
current service.

- '. . . the standards now generally attained by our pupils are
  neither as good as they can be, nor as good as they need to be if
  young people are to be equipped for the world of the twenty-first
  century.'
- '. . . the present spectrum of quality and the variations between
  schools are wider than is acceptable in a national system of
  school education based on 11 years of compulsory attendance.'
- 'A weakness found to a greater or lesser degree in about
  three-quarters of primary and middle schools is in curricular
  planning and its implementation.'
- 'In secondary schools there is little evidence of agreed
  curriculum policies directly influencing the school as a whole . . .
  Many departments still fail to translate their own, and the
  school's, declared aims and objectives into practical terms . . . '
- '. . . many children (in primary schools) are still given too little
  opportunity for work in the scientific, practical and aesthetic
  areas of the curriculum . . . '
- 'In about half of all (primary) classes much work in classrooms is
  so closely directed by the teacher that there is little opportunity
  either for oral discussion or for posing and solving practical
  problems. Pupils are given insufficient responsibility for
  pursuing their own enquiries and deciding how to tackle their
  work.'
- 'In virtually all (secondary) schools and departments there is
  often excessive direction by the teacher of pupils' work, and
  there are too many lessons where classwork and homework are
  unimaginatively set. Pupils need more opportunities to learn for
  themselves, to express their own views and to develop their
  ideas through discussion . . . . '
- 'Many teachers' judgements of pupils' potential and of their
  learning needs tend to reflect preconceptions about the
  capabilities of different categories of pupil. These preconceptions
  are often shared by parents and by the pupils themselves. As a
  result, expectations of pupils are insufficiently demanding at all
  levels of ability.'
- '. . . few (primary) schools or LEAs have formulated and
  implemented policies for assessment and record-keeping

designed to be used to ensure progress and continuity of learning for all pupils in all areas of the curriculum.'

■ 'Most (secondary) schools also still lack detailed assessment policies, which should be an integral part of the curriculum, not an optional extra.'

In order to tackle these weaknesses and to improve standards the Government identified, amongst others, the following areas of policy where action was required:

■ 'to secure greater clarity about the objectives and content of the curriculum;'
■ 'to reform the examination system and improve assessment so that they promote more effectively the objectives of the curriculum, the achievement of pupils, and the recording of those achievements.'

Breadth, balance, relevance, differentiation

Better Schools went on to discuss in detail the changes required to effect improvement. As a first step it would be necessary to obtain broad agreement about the objectives and content of the school curriculum, and several fundamental principles were offered:

■ 'the curriculum in both primary and secondary schools should be **broad**: as a whole and in its parts it should introduce the pupil to a wide range of areas of experience, knowledge and skill.'
■ 'the curriculum should be **balanced**: each area of the curriculum should be allotted sufficient time to make its specific contribution, but not so much that it squeezes out other essential areas.'
■ 'the curriculum should be **relevant**: all subjects should be taught in such a way as to make plain their link with the pupils' own experience and to bring out their applications and continuing value in adult life.'
■ 'there should be careful **differentiation**: what is taught and how it is taught need to be matched to pupils' abilities and aptitudes.'

The White Paper then stressed how vital it was 'that schools should always remember that preparation for working life is one of their principal functions. The economic stresses of our time and the pressures of international competition make it more necessary than ever before that Britain's work-force should possess the skills and attitudes, and display the understanding, the enterprise and adaptability that the pervasive impact of technological advance will increasingly demand.'

Going on to the primary curriculum, the White Paper stated that the content of the primary curriculum should make it possible for the primary phase to:

- 'place substantial emphasis on achieving competence in the use of language;'
- 'place substantial emphasis on achieving competence in mathematics;'
- 'introduce pupils to science;'
- 'lay the foundation of understanding in religious education, history and geography, and the nature and values of British society;'
- 'introduce the pupils to a range of activities in the arts;'
- 'provide opportunities throughout the curriculum for craft and practical work leading up to some experience of design and technology and of solving problems;'
- 'provide moral education, physical education and health education;'
- 'introduce pupils to the nature and use in school and in society of new technology;'
- 'give pupils some insights into the adult world, including how people earn their living.'

With respect to the secondary phase, 'during the first three years the curriculum should continue to be largely common to all pupils, but varied in pace and depth to reflect differences in ability and maturity. This principle should apply not only to English (and where appropriate Welsh), mathematics, religious education and physical education. It should also apply in substance, and irrespective of the timetable titles used, to science, where all pupils should study a balanced course through the three year period; to the humanities where both history and geography should be studied by all throughout; to aesthetic subjects, where all pupils should study, over the three years, music, art and drama on a worthwhile scale; and to practical subjects, where all pupils should be introduced to design and work in a range of materials in the subject areas of CDT and home economics. All pupils should be introduced to new technology and . . . the great majority of pupils should receive a course in a foreign language designed to be of lasting value.'

In the 4th and 5th secondary years, 'every pupil needs to continue . . . with English, mathematics, science and, save in exceptional circumstances, with physical education or games; should study elements drawn from both the humanities and the arts; and should take part in practical and technological work in a number of subjects, for example in CDT and not least in science. Most pupils should also continue with a foreign language.'

Although the White Paper talked largely in subject terms, it stated that 'such a description implies no particular view of timetabling or teaching approach. Nor does it deny that learning involves the mastery of processes as well as the acquisition of knowledge, skills and understanding.'

Thus *Better Schools* laid the foundations on which an agreed curriculum, both primary and secondary, could be built. The Government was looking to formulate national objectives for the curriculum which would provide a policy framework within which LEAs and schools would operate. However, there was to be a very definite limit to the extent of the role of the Secretary of State. 'For example, it would not in the view of the Government be right for the Secretaries of State's policy for the range and pattern of the 5-16 curriculum to amount to the determination of national syllabuses for that period.'

Curriculum policy and the 1986 Education Act

Building on the White Paper *Better Schools*, the 1986 Education Act laid curriculum responsibilities on the LEAs, Governing Bodies and headteachers. In meeting these responsibilities, they were each required to consider the range and balance of the secular curriculum and the balance between its different components.

The Act laid down duties as follows:

- for the LEA − to determine and keep under review their policy in relation to the secular curriculum for schools under their control;
- for the Governing Body − to consider the policy of the LEA and to establish the aims of the secular curriculum for the school;

- for the headteacher – to determine and organise the secular curriculum and to secure the delivery of that curriculum within the school. The curriculum to be followed was to be compatible with the LEA curriculum statement, or, where it differed, to differ in line with the stated aims of the Governing Body.

The move to a National Curriculum

With the appointment of Kenneth Baker as Secretary of State in 1986, perceptions as to how far there should be prescription from the centre began to change. For the first time, a nationally determined core curriculum began to be a live agenda item. Within twelve months the Conservative Party was able to promise in its Manifesto for the June 1987 General Election that, should it be returned to power, 'we will establish a National Core Curriculum. It is vital that all pupils between the ages of 5 and 16 study a basic range of subjects – including maths, English and science. In each of these basic subjects syllabuses will be published and attainment levels set so that the progress of pupils can be assessed at around ages 7, 11 and 14, and in preparation for the GCSE at 16. Parents, teachers and pupils will then know how well each child is doing. We will consult widely among those concerned in establishing the curriculum.'

The Consultation Document on the National Curriculum

Only a month after its election victory, the Government published a consultation document: *The National Curriculum 5-16*. This consultation document acknowledged the measure of agreement about, and support for, the aims of education as set out in *Better Schools*. It noted that many LEAs and schools had made important advances towards achieving a good curriculum for pupils aged 5-16.

The document then continued: 'But progress has been variable, uncertain and often slow. Improvements have been made, some standards of attainment have risen. But some improvement is not enough. We must raise standards consistently, and at least as quickly as they are rising in competitor countries . . . The Government now wishes to move ahead at a faster pace to ensure that this happens and to secure for all pupils in maintained schools a curriculum which equips them with the knowledge, skills and understanding that they need for adult life and employment.'

The consultation document claimed that a national curriculum backed by clear assessment arrangements would help to raise standards of attainment by:

- 'ensuring that all pupils study a broad and balanced range of subjects throughout their compulsory schooling and do not drop too early studies which may stand them in good stead later;'
- 'setting clear objectives for what children over the full range of ability should be able to achieve;'
- 'ensuring that all pupils . . . have access to broadly the same good and relevant curriculum and programmes of study;'
- 'checking on progress towards those objectives and performance achieved at various stages, so that pupils can be stretched further when they are doing well and given more help when they are not.'

In addition to raising standards, a national curriculum would:

- 'secure that the curriculum offered in all maintained schools has sufficient in common to enable children to move from one area of the country to another with minimum disruption to their education. It will also help children's progression within and between primary and secondary education (and on to further and higher education) and will help to secure the continuity and coherence which is too often lacking in what they are taught.'
- 'enable schools to be more accountable for the education they offer their pupils, individually and collectively . . . It will help alert teachers to problems experienced by individual children so that they can be given special attention . . . LEAs will be better placed to assess the strengths and weaknesses of the schools they maintain . . . Employers too will have a better idea of what a school-leaver will have studied and learnt at school.'

The document continued: 'The Government has concluded that these advantages and consistent improvement in standards can be guaranteed only within a national framework for the secular curriculum. To be effective, that must be backed by law . . . '

Thus, eleven years after the first musings of Prime Minister Callaghan, the edifice of the national curriculum outlined in the remainder of this book began to be built. The walls of the secret garden of the curriculum were about to be finally demolished.

2 The General Requirements

What is meant by the term 'The National Curriculum'?

The National Curriculum is the curriculum laid down by the Government. It is to be studied:

- by all pupils;
- in schools in the state sector;
- during the period of compulsory schooling (i.e. from the age of 5 to 16.)

The relevant legislation is contained in the Education Reform Act.

What are the provisions of the Education Reform Act?

The Education Reform Act is a large piece of legislation covering the following matters:

- the National Curriculum;
- religious education and collective worship;
- numbers of pupils who may be admitted to each school;
- local management of schools (The delegation to schools of management responsibility, including that for finance);
- Grant Maintained Schools (opting out);
- provision and funding of Higher and Further Education;
- the abolition of the ILEA and the transfer of responsibility for education to the inner London Boroughs.

The concern of this book is the National Curriculum which is dealt with in Chapter 1 of the Act.

When does the Education Reform Act come into effect?

The Education Reform Act was passed by Parliament and given Royal Assent in July 1988. The provisions in the Act will gradually come on stream in accordance with timetables laid down in the Act or in accordance with Government decisions taken under authority delegated by the Act. The first parts of the National Curriculum provisions will come into effect very quickly (see Chapters 7 and 8 of this book). The Secretary of State must establish all of the National Curriculum as soon as it is reasonably practicable to do so, but it is likely to be many years before the Act is fully implemented with respect to all the subjects in the National Curriculum.

To which schools does the National Curriculum apply?

The National Curriculum applies to all pupils of compulsory school age (i.e. 5-16) being educated in schools in the maintained (state) sector. This **includes** any Grant Maintained (opted out) schools but it does **not include** the following:

- nursery schools;
- nursery classes in primary schools;
- city technology colleges (CTCs);
- schools in the independent sector.

However, it is expected that many independent schools will choose to arrange their curriculum in accordance with the National Curriculum provisions and to submit their pupils for the National Assessments at the prescribed ages.

Are there any pupils to whom the National Curriculum does NOT apply?

As explained above, the National Curriculum should apply to all pupils aged 5-16 who are being educated in the state sector. However the Education Reform Act does allow for exceptions to this.

Firstly, parts of the National Curriculum requirements may be lifted or modified in specified cases or circumstances, under regulations to be made by the Secretary of State. For example, where the National Curriculum requires certain kinds of practical work, alternative arrangements might be prescribed in the interests of safe working for those with physical disabilities.

Secondly, where a pupil with special educational needs is statemented under the 1981 Act, the special educational provision specified in the statement may allow for exclusion from, or modification of, the provisions of the National Curriculum if they are inappropriate for the pupil concerned.

Thirdly, headteachers will be allowed to make temporary exemptions for individual pupils who are not statemented. The Secretary of State is empowered by the Act to make the necessary regulations and these will enable headteachers to decide for an individual pupil:

either that the National Curriculum shall not apply;
or that the National Curriculum shall apply with specified modifications.

The exemption or modification will apply for a maximum of six months in the first instance. It is hoped that at the end of that period the pupil might be able to return to an education which fully implements the requirements of the National Curriculum. Alternatively the period might be used to decide that special educational provision for the pupil needs to be made under the terms of the 1981 Act.

What are the general curricular provisions of the Act?

The curriculum for a maintained school has to satisfy the requirements of the Act which are that the curriculum should be **balanced** and **broadly based** and should:

- promote the spiritual, moral, cultural, mental and physical development of the pupil;
- prepare the pupils for the opportunities, responsibilities and experiences of adult life.

The basic curriculum is to include:

- provison for religious education;
- the National Curriculum.

What are the objectives of these curricular provisions?

The objectives of the school curriculum are that it should be:

- **broad** so that it introduces each pupil to a wide range of concepts, experience, knowledge and skills and promotes spiritual, moral, cultural, mental and physical development;
- **balanced** so that each area of the broad curriculum is allowed sufficient time for its contribution to be effective;
- **relevant** so that all subjects contribute to a sound general education which prepares pupils for the opportunities, responsibilities and experiences of adult life;
- **differentiated** so that what is taught and how it is taught is matched to and develops individual pupils' abilities and aptitudes.

The curriculum is to further the aims of the Technical and Vocational Education Initiative − making the curriculum more practical and relevant to adult and working life and emphasising personal development, careers guidance and work experience.

The curriculum should also reflect the culturally diverse society to which pupils belong and in which they will grow up. The curriculum should prepare them for all aspects of adulthood − in the home and as a parent; in employment; and in the community and society, locally, nationally and internationally.

What are the subjects in the National Curriculum?

The National Curriculum consists of a number of **core** and **foundation** subjects as listed in Table 1.

Photocopy

TABLE 1: THE CORE AND FOUNDATION SUBJECTS

Core Subjects	Foundation Subjects
Mathematics English Science Welsh (for schools in Wales which are Welsh-speaking schools)	History Geography *Technology Music Art Physical Education A modern foreign language (for pupils 11-16) Welsh (for schools in Wales which are non-Welsh speaking schools)
*Although 'Technology' is the subject name used in the Act, the title 'Design and Technology' is the one likely to be adopted for this curriculum area.	

What about religious education?

The basic curriculum must include a provision for religious education for all children. It is worth stressing that this includes pupils who are over the age of compulsory education: sixth form pupils in a secondary school and students attending a sixth form college. This religious education is to reflect the fact that the religious traditions of Great Britain are in the main Christian. However, schools are to take account also of the teaching and practices of the other principal religions represented in Great Britain.

In addition, the Act requires that all pupils who attend a maintained school (other than special schools) take part in a collective act of worship. This means that on each school day every pupil should be involved in an act of worship with other pupils. The 1944 Education Act already required that pupils take part in daily collective worship, with all the pupils at the school assembling at the same time. While most primary schools are able to do this, and indeed many do so, the Act created great difficulties for larger secondary schools. Many secondary schools simply have no space large enough to accommodate all its pupils at the same time. It is

photocopy.

not surprising, therefore, that this part of the 1944 Act has fallen into disuse.

Where the Education Reform Act differs from the 1944 Act with regard to collective worship is in the requirement for a single daily assembly. The new Act will still permit a single act of collective worship, but as an alternative it will also allow a number of smaller assemblies. As a result, a pupil might be involved in collective worship as part of a whole school assembly, or a year group assembly or a form assembly. It will therefore be very much more difficult for schools to claim that they are unable to comply with the law.

The act of worship should be wholly or mainly of a broadly Christian character. However the Standing Advisory Council on Religious Education which the local education authority must establish has the power to allow schools dispensation on this matter.

Parents have the right for their child to be wholly or partly excused from attendance at religious worship. There is the right also for parents to withdraw their child from religious education.

Can the National Curriculum be changed?

The Secretary of State can change by Order the list of core and other foundation subjects, and the ages to which the various stages relate. However, any such proposals have to be the subject of full public consultation, followed by a resolution passed by both Houses of Parliament.

It is expected that much of the normal run of curriculum development in schools will be capable of being carried out within the framework specified for each subject. It is hoped that the framework will be sufficiently flexible to allow schools to devise and adopt suitable new approaches.

However, the Secretary of State has power to modify or lift temporarily some or all of the National Curriculum requirements in a particular school, or group of schools, so that curriculum development can be carried out. Applications will be accepted either from the school's governing body (with the LEA's agreement) or from the LEA (with the school's agreement). The application will have to state which statutory requirements need to be waived, the benefits sought by the school from such a waiver and the extent to which the benefits may be of wider relevance.

How much of the timetable will be taken up by the National Curriculum?

The Act requires that each of the core and foundation subjects be taught for **a reasonable time**. There will be no statutory definition of what a reasonable time is. In fact, the Act **forbids** the Secretary of State from requiring:

- that any particular period or periods of time should be allocated during any key stage to any programme of study or any part of it;
- that provision of any particular kind should be made in school timetables for the periods to be allocated to such teaching.

However, pupils will be expected to spend sufficient time in each core and foundation subject to enable them to undertake worthwhile study. In practice, the depth and breadth of the programmes of study and the level of difficulty of the attainment targets will to a large extent determine the time which must be devoted to particular subjects. Indeed, in giving guidance to the subject working groups which he established to make proposals in the first core and foundation subjects, the Secretary of State indicated the approximate amount of time which might reasonably be spent on each subject. This is shown in Table 2.

In total, it is expected that at least 70-80% of the timetable will be taken up by the core and other foundation subjects.

TABLE 2: PERIODS PER WEEK IN EACH KEY STAGE (ASSUMING
A 40 PERIOD WEEK)

	Stage One (Ages 5-7)	**Stage Two** (Ages 7-11)	**Stage Three** (Ages 11-14)	**Stage Four** (Ages 14-16)
English	8	8	6	5
Mathematics	8	8	4	4
Science	} 5	} 5	8	8*
Technology			2-4	2
History	3-4	3-4	3-4	2

* Although there is an option in the Statutory Order for schools to follow a
reduced course in science, the Secretary of State has made it clear that he hopes
that the majority of pupils will follow the fuller option which implies eight
periods of study per week.

What about subjects which are NOT part of the National Curriculum?

If up to 80 per cent of the curricular time available has to be
devoted to the teaching and learning of core and foundation
subjects, 20-30 per cent of the time will remain for other activities.
This may be used in one of two ways:

■ broadening or deepening study in core or other foundation
subjects beyond what is immediately required by the statutory
programmes of study and attainment targets;
■ studying subjects outside the National Curriculum.

There will therefore be scope for schools to continue to provide
courses in subjects outside the National Curriculum. However,
there will be two serious constraints:

■ there is unlikely to be time for an individual pupil to take more
than two additional full subjects outside the National
Curriculum (and for many pupils the National Curriculum will
constitute a full timetable);

■ there will be a limit to the number of additional subjects which a
school will able to staff and resource.

In this situation, some subjects currently in the pre-16 curriculum are likely to disappear from the timetable in many schools. Other subjects might be subsumed within core or foundation subjects: for instance, home economics and business studies could become options within technology. In other curriculum areas, a modular approach might preserve individual subjects as units within a broad syllabus. For instance, sociology could form part of a modular humanities course which in addition allowed the programmes of study and attainment targets in geography and history to be met.

It must be remembered, however, that where a course provided for pupils of compulsory school age leads to an external qualification, that qualification and the associated syllabus must be approved by the Secretary of State or by a body designated by him. This could limit in some cases the courses which schools will wish to offer, especially during the Fourth Key Stage.

What are cross-curricular themes and how will these be encompassed within the National Curriculum?

In the Education Reform Act, the National Curriculum is described purely in subject terms. However, it has always been the Government's intention that there shall also be opportunities for working across the curriculum where this is appropriate. The report *The National Curriculum 5-16: A Consultation Document* states:

> '. . . there are a number of subjects or themes such as health education and use of information technology, which can be taught through other subjects . . . It is proposed that such subjects or themes should be taught through the foundation subjects, so that they can be accommodated within the curriculum but without crowding out the essential subjects.'

In giving guidance to each of the subject working groups which he has established, the Secretary of State has asked to be informed about the place of such 'cross-curricular' subjects, themes and skills within the context of the subject concerned.

In practice, there are likely to be two aspects of cross-curricularity which the National Curriculum will seek to exploit.

The first aspect will seek to identify the commonality and inter-relationships between subjects. For instance, students could be shown how the skills learnt in one subject apply to other parts of the Curriculum. Thus the skills associated with measure, or the manipulation and interpretation of data, first learnt in the mathematics classroom, could be applied in the science, geography and history classrooms.

This aspect may be reinforced by the introduction of records of achievement. The Report of the Records of Achievement National Steering Committee published in January, 1989, recommended that records of achievement be introduced for all pupils, at least in the secondary sector, by the early 1990s. The Report also identified five general skills which run across the curriculum:

- information handling;
- organising work;
- communication skills;
- working with others;
- personal qualities.

The second aspect will concern the identification of themes which straddle the curriculum and to which many of the individual core and other foundation subjects can contribute. To date, a number of themes have been identified, although the following list is unlikely to be exhaustive:

- economic awareness;
- consumer affairs;
- health education;
- information technology;
- media studies;
- careers education;
- industrial awareness;
- environmental issues.

At the present time, it is not clear how schools will be expected to arrange for the delivery of such themes nor whether there will be any formal assessment requirement.

3 The Format

What will the National Curriculum comprise?

The National Curriculum will comprise the core and other foundation subjects. Remember that the core subjects are:

- English;
- mathematics;
- science;
- Welsh, in Welsh-speaking schools.

The other foundation subjects are:

- technology;
- geography;
- history;
- a modern foreign language (for pupils 11-16);
- art;
- music;
- physical education;
- Welsh, in schools in Wales which are not Welsh-speaking.

What is the basic structure of the National Curriculum within each subject?

Each subject in the National Curriculum is structured using the concepts of:

- attainment targets;
- programmes of study;
- levels;
- profile components;
- key stages.

This chapter looks in detail at each of these concepts. In summary, however:

- each subject is divided into a number of **attainment targets**, specified in terms of knowledge, skills and understanding;
- within each attainment target, or group of attainment targets, there is an associated **programme of study** (i.e. syllabus or subject content);
- each attainment target is assessed in terms of ten **levels**;
- for reporting purposes, the attainment targets are grouped into **profile components**;
- assessment and reporting take place at the end of each **key stage**. There are four key stages:

first key stage: ages 5-7
second key stage: ages 7-11
third key stage: ages 11-14
fourth key stage: ages 14-16

Now let us look at each of these concepts in more detail.

What are attainment targets?

Section 2 of the Education Reform Act 1988 defines attainment targets as:

'the knowledge, skills and understanding which pupils of different abilities and maturities are expected to have by the end of each key stage.'

The Secretary of State gives this additional information to each subject working group:

'By "attainment targets" I have in mind clearly specified objectives for what pupils should know, understand and be able to do, which can be related to what might be expected of pupils of different abilities and maturities at or around the end of the academic year in which they reach the ages of 7, 11, 14 and 16. It is essential that attainment targets provide specific enough objectives for pupils, teachers, parents and others to have a clear idea of what is expected and to produce a sound basis for assessment and testing. They should represent current best practice and achievements.'

Examples of attainment targets produced so far are:

- algebra: recognise and use functions, formulae, equations and inequalities (in **mathematics**);
- making new materials: pupils should develop their knowledge and understanding of the process of changing materials by chemical reaction and the way this is used in the manufacture of new materials (in **science**);
- speaking and listening: pupils should demonstrate their understanding of the spoken word and the capacity to express themselves effectively in a variety of speaking and listening activities, matching style and response to audience and purpose (in **English**);
- make artefacts and systems: working to a scheme derived from their previously developed design, pupils should be able to identify, manage and use appropriate resources, including both knowledge and processes, in order to make an artefact or system (in **design and technology**).

The process by which attainment targets and programmes of study are specified allows for considerable flexibility with regard to the degree of detail prescribed. The Secretary of State intends that attainment targets and programmes of study should be more detailed for the core subjects than for the other foundation subjects. For art, music and physical education, the requirements are expected to be very broad, with more detail given in non-statutory guidelines.

Each attainment target will be defined in more detailed statements of attainment at up to ten levels.

What are levels of attainment?

Attainment targets and programmes of study are intended to be appropriate for pupils of different abilities and maturities. The Task Group on Assessment and Testing (TGAT) recommended that attainment should be assessed on a ten level scale covering the full period of compulsory education — for children from 5 to 16 years. The Government has accepted this recommendation. Attainment targets are thus to be defined by detailed statements of attainment at each of ten levels. Progress from one level of attainment to the next will reflect development according to age and time in schooling and also different abilities and aptitudes of pupils.

There will be no requirement for any particular level to be reached by a particular age. However, teachers will be expected to know what levels of attainment pupils are generally likely to reach at particular ages and to set pupils objectives which reflect these.

Examples of levels of attainment developed so far are:

- AT6 algebra: level 2
  understand the use of a symbol to stand for an unknown number (in **mathematics**);
- AT7 making new materials: level 4
  know that when a chemical reaction occurs, new materials are formed;
  know that an important feature of manufacture is the conversion of raw materials, by chemical reactions, into useful products (in **science**);
- writing AT3 − handwriting: level 2
  produce properly oriented and mainly legible upper and lower case letters in one style (e.g. printed);
  use upper and lower case letters consistently, (i.e. not randomly mixed within words);
  use ascenders and descenders clearly (in **English**).

What are programmes of study?

Section 2 of the Act defines programmes of study as:

'the matters, skills and processes which are required to be taught to pupils of different abilities and maturities during each key stage.'

In his supplementary guidance to the subject working groups, the Secretary of State requires:

'programmes of study to provide a detailed description of the content, skills and processes which all pupils need to be taught so that they can develop the knowledge and understanding they will need to progress through school and eventually to adult life and employment . . . .'

He went on to say that the programmes of study needed:

'to be set within an outline or overall map'

of the subject which set out what might be expected of pupils of different abilities.

Teachers' autonomy is recognised in the final paragraph:

'Within the overall programme of study, the Government's intention is that there must be space to accommodate the enterprise of teachers, offering them sufficient flexibility in the choice of content to adapt what they teach to the needs of the individual pupil.'

What are profile components?

Following the report of the Task Group on Assessment and Testing, the Government agreed to adopt a number of principles related to assessment. These included the intention that:

'Pupils' performance in relation to attainment targets should be assessed and reported on at ages 7, 11, 14 and 16. Attainment targets should be grouped for this purpose to make the assessment and reporting manageable.'

These groupings of attainment targets are known as profile components. It is in terms of these profile components that pupils' progress in the various foundation subjects will be measured and reported.

TGAT recommended that each subject should report a small number of profile components 'preferably no more than four and never more than six.' In practice, the number of profile components, in the subjects that have reported so far, has been very small – two each in the case of science and mathematics, and three in primary English. The interim report of the design and technology working group recommended a single profile component.

TGAT also recommended cross-curricular profile components:

'Wherever possible, one or more components should have more general application across the curriculum: for these a single common specification should be adopted in each of the subjects concerned.'

Although it is as yet early days, there is no evidence among the reports of the subject working groups that such developments are in fact taking place.

What are the key stages?

The National Curriculum applies to all pupils of compulsory school age who are being educated in maintained schools. In other words it operates from the ages of 5 to 16. This age range has been divided into **four key stages** as follows:

- first key stage: ages 5-7

- second key stage: ages 7-11

- third key stage: ages 11-14

- fourth key stage: ages 14-16

A stage is defined as **beginning** at the start of the school year in which the majority of the pupils in the teaching group attain the given age. Thus for example the third key stage starts at the beginning of the academic year in which the majority of pupils in the class reach the age of 12.

Key stage 1 for a child starts when he/she becomes of compulsory school age – the start of the term **following** his/her fifth birthday. But **for the 1989-90 school year only,** the attainment targets and programmes of study for mathematics, science and English will apply to pupils from the start of the school year after they have reached compulsory school age.

A stage is defined as **ending** at the end of the school year in which the majority of pupils in the teaching group attain the given age. Thus for example the third key stage ends at the end of the academic year in which most pupils in the class reach the age of 14.

The Secretary of State may alter the dividing age between the **first** and **second** stage for any subject. However, there is no indication at the moment that this provision will be used i.e. the end of the first key stage is likely to remain at 7 for most subjects.

A key stage is defined with reference to **the age of the majority of pupils** in a teaching group. An individual pupil might well be younger or older. For instance, a mathematically gifted girl aged 13 will be able to start the fourth key stage in mathematics if she is put in a teaching group where the majority of children will reach the age of 15 during that school year. A pupil can therefore be taught with another age group for one or more subject areas where appropriate, whilst remaining with his or her peer group for other subjects.

It is possible that some teaching groups will span more than one age group. Headteachers will then have discretion to treat pupils according to their individual chronological ages rather than the age of the majority of the teaching groups, so that where it is necessary or desirable these pupils can be treated differently.

For the majority of children, the end of the second key stage will coincide with the move from primary to secondary school. However, in those local education authorities in which a middle school system operates, the end of the second key stage will fall part way through the pupil's time at the middle school. Thus both the middle and the secondary schools will be responsible for teaching the third key stage. In these situations it will be particularly important that arrangements are made for smooth progression from one school to another.

4 The Production

What is the process for producing the National Curriculum?

This chapter looks in detail at the process of producing the National Curriculum. However, the procedure is summarised schematically in Table 3.

TABLE 3: THE PROCESS FOR PRODUCING THE NATIONAL CURRICULUM

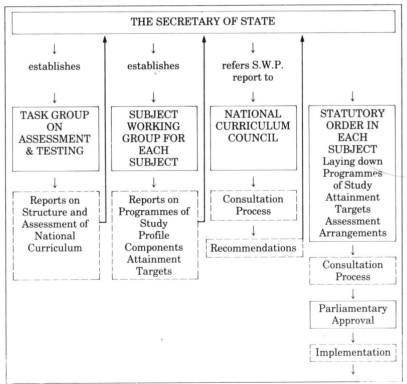

Whose responsibility is it to establish the National Curriculum?

Section 4 of the Education Reform Act 1988 states that:

'(1) It shall be the duty of the Secretary of State so to exercise the powers conferred by subsection (2) below as:
   (a) to establish a complete National Curriculum as soon as it is reasonably practicable (taking first the core subjects and then the other foundation subjects); and
   (b) to revise that Curriculum whenever he considers it necessary or expedient to do so.

(2) The Secretary of State may by order specify in relation to each of the foundation subjects:
   (a) such attainment targets;
   (b) such programmes of study; and
   (c) such assessment arrangements;
   as he considers appropriate for that subject.'

Clearly, the responsibility is the Secretary of State's. However, in discharging that responsibility, Kenneth Baker has sought the assistance of other bodies; the Task Group on Assessment and Testing, the National Curriculum Council, the School Examinations and Assessment Council and, for each core and other foundation subject, a subject working group.

What is the role of the Task Group on Assessment and Testing?

In July 1987, the Secretary of State set up a working group to look at assessment within the proposed National Curriculum. It was entitled the Task Group on Assessment and Testing. Its membership included representatives of the examinations and assessment establishment − from the Secondary Examinations Council, the City and Guilds of London Institute and the National Foundation for Educational Research − as well as educationalists and others. It was chaired by Professor Paul Black of King's College, London.

Its terms of reference were:

- to advise on the practical considerations which should govern all assessment including testing of attainment at the end of each of the four key stages;
- to take into account the need not to increase calls on teachers' and pupils' time for activities which do not directly promote learning and to limit costs;
- to advise on the possibility of staging the introduction of assessment – including testing – to reflect the need for the implementation process to be manageable and for teachers to be adequately trained;
- to report its conclusions to the Secretary of State by Christmas 1987.

In advising on assessment, the group was asked to comment on:

- the marking scales and kinds of assessment and testing to be used;
- the need for differentiation;
- the roles of formative and diagnostic testing;
- the uses to which assessment results should be put;
- moderation;
- publication and other services needed to support the system of assessment.

The overall aim was to secure:

'. . . assessment and testing arrangements which are simple to administer, understandable by all in and outside the education service, cost-effective, and supportive of learning in schools.'

The Task Group on Assessment and Testing produced its report on 24 December 1987. Its chairman confirmed that the group had been able to deal with the issues raised in its terms of reference, with the exception of the various services and arrangements needed to support the assessment system it had recommended. The group proposed that it report on this issue about two months later. At the same time it would provide fuller elaboration on other issues.

Rather later than it had proposed, the group published three supplementary reports on 25 March 1988. The first supplementary report was in response to the need to explain more fully the implications of some of the recommendations in the main report.

The second dealt with the application of the recommendations to the various foundation subjects, and the third provided recommendations about the system of support that the assessment arrangements would require.

In an announcement to Parliament on 7 June 1988, Kenneth Baker gave the Government's decisions on the Task Group on Assessment and Testing's recommendations. These were in the form of a number of principles which would form the basis of a national system of assessment and testing related to the National Curriculum attainment targets:

- attainment targets would establish what children should be expected to know, understand and do at the ages of 7, 11, 14 and 16, and would enable progress to be measured against national standards;
- performance in relation to attainment targets would be assessed and reported on at ages 7, 11, 14 and 16. Attainment targets would be grouped – into profile components – to make the assessment and reporting manageable;
- levels of attainment would be measured on a ten point scale covering the full 5 to 16 age range;
- assessment would be by a combination of national external tests and teacher assessments. At 16, the main form of assessment, especially in English, mathematics and science, would be the GCSE;
- assessment results would be used formatively and summatively;
- individual pupils' results would not be published, but would be given to parents. Aggregated results at 11, 14 and 16 would be published, but at 7 there would be no legal requirement for schools to publish such results;
- teacher assessments would be compared with results of the national tests and with the judgements of other teachers in order to safeguard standards.

The Secretary of State did express concern over the suggestions on moderation arrangements made by the Task Group on Assessment and Testing in its third supplementary report; he felt that these were 'complicated and costly'. He announced the he would be having further discussions on the issues involved with the School Examinations and Assessment Council and the National Curriculum Council, as well as with the local education authorities, examining groups and other appropriate organisations.

What is the role of the National Curriculum Council?

Under Section 14 of the Act, the Secretary of State has set up the National Curriculum Council (in Wales, the Curriculum Council for Wales).

The Council was established in August 1988, under the chairmanship of Mr Duncan Graham, with the following statutory functions:

- to keep all aspects of the curriculum for maintained schools under review;
- to advise the Secretary of State on such matters concerned with the curriculum for maintained schools as he may refer to it or as he may see fit;
- to advise the Secretary of State on, and if so requested by him to carry out, programmes of research and development for purposes connected with the curriculum for schools;
- to publish and disseminate, and to assist in the publication and dissemination of, information relating to the curriculum for schools;
- to carry out such ancillary activities as the Secretary of State may direct.

The NCC's responsibilities therefore include all aspects of the curriculum, not just for the age range and subjects covered by the National Curriculum. It has, however, a special responsibility for the National Curriculum.

The Education Reform Act provides for the National Curriculum to apply differently in different circumstances, and it will be one of the NCC's responsibilities to advise the Secretary of State on how this flexibility should be applied.

The Council will also recommend new curriculum development projects which it believes are needed in relation to the introduction of the National Curriculum as well as establishing arrangements to take part in evaluating its introduction.

Perhaps its major role will be with regard to consultation and reporting. The Act provides for consultation on the proposals for attainment targets and programmes of study to be carried out by the NCC. These proposals have so far derived from the reports of the subject working groups established by the Secretary of State.

The Council is required to consult associations of local education authorities, bodies representing school governors, teacher organisations and others whom the NCC decide are appropriate. In the case of the proposals for mathematics and science, the NCC consulted over 400 organisations, as well as sending copies of the reports to all maintained schools. When the consultation period is over, the NCC reports to the Secretary of State, giving a summary of the views expressed and giving its recommendations on the proposals. In addition, it may give any other advice relating to the proposals as it sees fit.

Early tasks for the NCC include consulting and advising on:

- the in-service training which teachers will need to introduce the National Curriculum;
- arrangements for exceptions to National Curriculum requirements in specified cases and circumstances, including those with special educational needs;
- which modern foreign languages can be offered as foundation subjects;
- arrangements for the operation of local complaints machinery;
- what information should be made available to parents and other bodies.

What is the role of the School Examinations and Assessment Council?

Under Section 14 of the Act, the Secretary of State has also established the School Examinations and Assessment Council (SEAC). The Council was set up, in August 1988, under the chairmanship of Philip Halsey to advise the Secretary of State on assessment and examinations.

The functions of the SEAC are as follows:

- to keep all aspects of examinations and assessment under review;
- to advise the Secretary of State on such matters concerned with examinations and assessment as he may refer to it or as it may see fit;
- to advise the Secretary of State on, and if so requested by him assist him to carry out, programmes of research and development for purposes connected with examinations and assessment;

- to publish and disseminate, and to assist in the publication and dissemination of, information relating to examinations and assessment;
- to make arrangements with appropriate bodies for the moderation of assessments made in pursuance of assessment arrangements;
- to advise the Secretary of State on the exercise of his powers under Section 5(1) of the Act (approval of qualifications);
- to carry out such ancillary activities as the Secretary of State may direct.

The first tasks of the Council include:

- sending out tenders for the development of standard assessment tasks for pupils at the end of the first key stage of the National Curriculum;
- advising on the implementation and operation of the assessment system;
- advising on the statutory approval of qualifications to be offered to pupils of compulsory school age;
- reviewing the experience of the first GCSE courses and examinations.

What do the subject working groups do?

For each of the foundation subjects, the Secretary of State appoints a subject working group to advise on attainment targets and programmes of study. The membership of each working group includes educationalists – teachers, advisers, Local Education Authority officers, university lecturers – and others with particular knowledge of the subject.

Once appointed, the subject working group is given its terms of reference, followed by more detailed guidance. The terms of reference require the working group firstly to submit an interim report to the Secretary of State outlining:

- the contribution which the subject should make to the overall school curriculum and how that will inform the working group's thinking about attainment targets and programmes of study;
- its provisional thinking about the knowledge, skills and understanding which pupils of different abilities and maturities should be expected to have attained and be able to demonstrate

at key ages; and the profile components into which attainment targets should be grouped;
- its thinking about the programmes of study which would be consistent with the provisionally identified attainment targets.

The working group is also given the date by which it must submit its final report setting out and justifying its final recommendations on attainment targets and programmes of study.

What is the timetable for the subject working groups?

Mathematics and science   The first subject working groups to be established were in mathematics and science. They were appointed by Kenneth Baker in July 1987 and were given until the end of November 1987 to produce their interim reports, setting out their preliminary thoughts on a number of issues. These included attainment targets, programmes of study, assessment and implementation. The final reports for mathematics and science, containing the working groups' recommendations for attainment targets and programmes of study for all four key stages, were produced on 30 June 1988. Altogether, then, each working group sat for approximately one year before producing its final recommendations. The science working group, in addition to its work in science, also produced recommendations for technology in the first two key stages – for 5 to 11 year olds.

English   In April 1988 the Secretary of State appointed an English working group to advise on attainment targets and programmes of study. The group was required to report in two phases. The first report, relating to primary English – the first two key stages – was produced on 30 September 1988. The report dealing with the third and fourth key stages was to be produced in May 1989. The working group of the Kingman Committee, in its terms of reference, were asked to build on the work which had been established to advise the Secretary of State on what pupils should know about language. Kingman had made recommendations about language at the ages of 7, 11 and 16, and the working group was required to take these into account when recommending attainment targets covering the grammatical structure of the English language.

Technology   The working group for technology was established in April 1988. The group in fact adopted the term 'design and technology' to describe the area of the curriculum that it would consider. Its terms of reference also asked the group to provide a focus for the development of Information Technology awareness and in order to do so recommend attainment targets and programmes of study related to IT and computer skills. The working group produced its interim report on 9 November 1988. The final report is due to be produced in May 1989. In its final report, the group were asked to:

- bring out how design and technology can contribute to the development of other curriculum themes, skills and personal qualities;
- consider whether any aspects of design would need to be covered in other curricular areas;
- decide whether any modifications would be needed for pupils with special educational needs;
- ensure that its recommendations were consistent with those of the working groups for English and, especially, mathematics and science;
- recommend whether pupils in key stage four should be allowed a choice between a general design and technology course and more specialised design and technological and business course options;
- consider further the number and grouping of attainment targets for Information Technology capability.

History   In January 1989, Kenneth Baker announced an outline timetable of work on the remaining foundation subjects. At the same time, he set up the working group for history. The group was to begin its work at once, and would produce an interim report in July 1989. Its final report is to be produced in December 1989.

Other foundation subjects   In January 1989, the Secretary of State also gave the following outline timetable for the other foundation subjects:

- the geography working group to be established by the Easter of 1989;
- the modern foreign languages working group to be set up in July 1989;
- arrangements for the consideration of the content of guidelines for music, art and physical education to be set up in June 1990.

_____

What are the arrangements for consultation?

On receiving the final report of a subject working party, the Secretary of State produces proposals for attainment targets and programmes of study in that subject. He then refers his proposals to the National Curriculum Council, together with directions as to the date by which it is to report back to him.

The National Curriculum Council then gives notice of the proposals to a number of bodies. By statute these must include:

- associations of local education authorities;
- organisations representing the interests of school governing bodies;
- organisations representing schoolteachers.

In addition, the NCC must consult with 'any other persons with whom consultation appears to it to be desirable'. These may include:

- advisers' associations;
- assessment and validating bodies;
- careers associations;
- local education authorities;
- industry;
- parents' organisations;
- special educational needs organisations;
- religious bodies;
- agencies representing primary education;
- agencies representing post 16, higher and further education;
- subject bodies;
- agencies, organisations and other bodies.

The NCC must give the bodies consulted 'a reasonable opportunity of submitting evidence and representations as to the issues arising.' These issues include practicability, coverage, levels, precision, cross-curricular elements and mutual consistency with other subject proposals.

The Council produces a response form on which those consulted may express their views on the issues to be considered. After analysing the responses, the NCC produces advice and recommendations on the general issues, taking account of the consultation. In addition, the Council makes recommendations for attainment targets (and associated statements of attainment) and programmes of study.

_____

What happens after the consultation period?

When the NCC has reported to the Secretary of State, he must publish Draft Orders and send them to the Council and to each person consulted by the Council. He must allow a period of at least one month for the submission of evidence and representations concerning issues arising from the Draft Orders. After this period has expired, the Secretary of State may make Statutory Orders, with or without amendments. These Orders are then laid before Parliament and, if approved, are implemented according to the timetable determined by the Secretary of State.

5 Assessment

What are the general purposes of assessment?

There are four general purposes of assessment:

- **formative** – formative assessment is that which takes place during the teaching/learning process. Its purposes are to:
  - recognise and reinforce positive achievement;
  - identify and correct where learning has not been effective; and
  - plan the next stage of learning;
- **diagnostic** – diagnostic assessment is used when a student appears to have a learning problem. It enables:
  - the nature and causes of the learning difficulties to be identified; and
  - appropriate remedial help and guidance to be given;
- **summative** – summative assessment records the achievement of a student over a period of time in a systematic way. This enables a coherent report to be given to the student and his/her parents and to other people or institutions with a legitimate interest in the information;
- **evaluative** – evaluative assessment enables the effectiveness of the teaching/learning process to be judged. This allows appropriate action to be taken, whether by the individual teacher, the school or the LEA, to reinforce and share good practice, and to recognise and improve less effective practice.

What are the assessment requirements of the National Curriculum?

Pupils must be assessed in each core and other foundation subject at or near the end of each key stage. This is a requirement of the

Education Reform Act and the National Curriculum must specify the assessment arrangements in each subject. The term 'assess' is defined as including 'examine' and 'test'. The purpose is to find out what pupils have achieved in relation to the attainment targets for that stage.

How will the Act be interpreted with respect to assessment?

In his guidance to the Task Group on Assessment and Testing (TGAT), the Secretary of State mentioned the four purposes of assessment — formative, diagnostic, summative and evaluative — and then went on to say:

> 'I attach importance to all of these, and expect your recommendations to cover all. But . . . the main purpose of the national assessment, including testing, in relation to agreed attainment targets for National Curriculum foundation subjects will be to "show what a pupils has learnt and mastered, so as to enable teachers and parents to ensure that he or she is making adequate progress and to inform decisions about the next steps".'

The extent of the reporting of National Curriculum assessments, not only to pupils and parents, but also on an aggregated basis to LEAs and Government, means that there are strong summative and evaluative strands within the National Curriculum assessment purposes. Nevertheless, there is also an underlying emphasis on their formative qualities.

What will be the form of assessment?

The Education Reform Act allows the Secretary of State to specify in relation to each of the National Curriculum subjects 'such assessment arrangements as he considers appropriate for that subject.' Any relevant techniques could therefore be used — written examinations, oral or practical tests, extended coursework projects etc.

What will be the structure of the assessment?

There will be two main assessment components:

- Standard Assessment Tasks, which will be externally set and available on a national basis;
- Moderated Teacher Ratings, which will be based on teachers' assessment of pupils' achievement as evidenced during the course.

The Secretary of State established the Task Group on Assessment and Testing to recommend the structure and systems of assessment for the National Curriculum. In advising TGAT on its work, the Secretary of State said:

> 'The Group's recommendations must be practicable to implement and cost-effective. I hope that your recommendations will take account of the very considerable amount of assessment which is already carried out as a normal part of teaching and learning in our schools, and will recognise that all forms of assessment affect the teaching and learning assessed. I am looking for arrangements which, by supplementing the normal assessments made by teachers in the classroom with simply-administered tests, will offer a clear picture of how pupils, individually and collectively, are faring at each of the age points. Such arrangements should help to promote good teaching.'

In its report to the Secretary of State, TGAT responded as follows:

> 'A combination of teachers' ratings and standardised assessment tasks can engender confidence in the interpretation of achievement. The combination will facilitate fair sampling of the National Curriculum, coverage of different circumstances of assessment on different occasions, and a range of evidence as the basis of report. Individually the instruments are open to misinterpretation but in combination they minimise the risks.
>
> **We therefore recommend that the national assessment system is based on a combination of moderated teachers' ratings and standardised assessment tasks.'**

This has been accepted by the Government and formal assessment under national arrangements will therefore bring together the results of externally prescribed standard assessment tasks and of teacher assessments at the end of each key stage.

What will be the form of the Standard Assessment Tasks?

The Standard Assessment Tasks will comprise a mixture of standardised assessment instruments including tests, practical tasks and observations.

The TGAT report notes that standard assessments need not only be in the written form. The art of constructing good assessment tasks, it says, is to exploit a wide range of:
– methods of presenting the task;
– methods of working;
– ways in which pupils may respond.
This widens the range of pupils' abilities that the tasks reflect and so enhances their educational validity.

An advantage of using an expanded range of possibilities is that there need be no obvious discontinuity between teachers' own assessment of normal classroom work and the use by them of standard tasks. An open-ended task might be so well integrated into the teaching process that pupils would not be aware of any departure from normal classroom work. TGAT therefore recommends that standard assessment tasks should be so designed that flexibility of form and use is allowed wherever this can be consistent with national comparability of results.

In a later section of the report headed 'National tests must use a variety of methods', TGAT notes that some kinds of task are easier and cheaper to set and mark than others. But use of only one kind of assessment instrument in the interests of economy could lead to undue emphasis on some targets at the expense of others, threatening distortion of curriculum coverage. The report therefore argues for a broad range of assessment instruments sampling a broad range of attainment targets, which would in turn discourage the narrowing tendency to 'teach to the test'.

Therefore, as noted above, the Standard Assessment Tasks will comprise a mixture of standardised assessment instruments including tests, practical tasks and observations. It is thus hoped to minimise any possibility that the national assessment system will cause curriculum distortion.

There will however be differences in the style of the standard assessment tasks used at the various key stages which will reflect both the maturity of the pupils and the way in which the curriculum is likely to have been delivered.

_____

Who will set the Standard Assessment Tasks?

It will be the responsibility of the School Examinations and Assessment Council to oversee the production of Standard Assessment Tasks at the various key stages.

It is intended that the development shall be put out to tender and three contracts for the development of SATs for the first key stage were awarded in December 1988. In this case, the contracts were awarded to consortia which usually included partners with experience in examining and assessing, teacher training and publishing together with LEAs. The development will include piloting in a large sample of schools. INSET packages will also be created to assist the teachers in incorporating the administration and assessment of SATs into their classroom practice.

SEAC will be issuing similar tenders in due course for the development of SATs for the third, and then the second and fourth key stages.

_____

What will the Standard Assessment Tasks be like for 7 year olds?

With respect to the first key stage, TGAT states the following:

'Because of the immaturity of the 7 year old children and the practices normally found in schools, we consider that externally provided tasks should be no more than three in number for each child. They should seem to the children to be part of ordinary school work, though conducted in a standardised way by the teacher. The tasks should not be differentiated according to levels of difficulty, but should be so constructed that children's performances on them can be related to the National Curriculum attainment targets. The topics should be selected by the teacher from item banks so that the matter on which the tasks are based will be within the children's general experience. The three tasks should be drawn from an item bank so as to allow the children to demonstrate clearly the stages reached in

literacy and numeracy and the range of other skills deemed
appropriate within the National Curriculum . . . Across a
balanced set of three such tasks it will be possible to appraise all
of the appropriate components on several occasions and in
several different contexts.'

The report then points out that at the age of 7 a proportion of the
children will not even be literate. This has to be allowed for in the
standard procedures laid down for the assessment tasks. Certainly
children must not be given a sense of failure because they are
unable to respond, and teachers must be allowed to give help under
prescribed circumstances.

Tenders for the construction of SATs for 7 year olds were issued by
the School Examinations and Assessment Council in December
1988. The following were points made in the brief to those wishing
to tender for the work:

- The SATs for 1991 should test knowledge, skill and
  understanding across the range of assessment targets for
  mathematics, science and English. For 1992 (the first year in
  which results will be reported), the SATs should also include
  design and technology;
- The SATs should be of the kind proposed by TGAT – packages of
  tasks administered through a range of modes. Their purpose is
  to be both formative and summative;
- The SATs for the national assessment should comprise a choice
  of three prescribed tasks for each child; each task to be designed
  to give opportunities for systematic assessment of competence in
  the relevant profile components. The aim is to cover the
  maximum practical number of attainment targets in the
  minimum number of SATs; and to cover some attainment
  targets from each profile component in each SAT;
- Individual schools and teachers are to be given a choice of SATs
  to administer to accord with their own teaching programmes;
  but that choice will be constrained to ensure that the SATs they
  select adequately cover the range of assessment targets and
  provide sufficient information on each profile component;
- SATs should be capable of being administered by teachers as a
  natural part of their normal (and frequently cross-curricular)
  mode of teaching. The SATs should require only those resources
  that are normally available in a primary school;

- The SATs will be constructed so that performance can be measured in terms of the first three levels on the ten level TGAT scale. There will also be scope for pupils to demonstrate attainment beyond level 3 where they can;
- Attainment targets will be assessed by a plurality of measures, using as appropriate written, oral, practical and graphic work done individually or in groups. Some written work will be included in each profile component but not necesssarily within each attainment target;
- SATs are to avoid ethnic, cultural and gender bias. Their use should not be inhibited by translation into a foreign language and they should not contain material which would disadvantage pupils from ethnic minorities.

What will the Standard Assessment Tasks be like for 11 year olds?

The TGAT Report notes that at the age of 11, children are likely to be working in a mixture of topic and subject modes. Some assessments may be required in a subject context, especially since secondary schools may require information that can be linked to a subject analysis of the curriculum. However, there is a danger of over-burdening teachers at this age if all aspects of the curriculum are tested exhaustively. TGAT therefore only suggests tentative solutions, pending advice from the subject working groups.

Possible solutions might include:

- concentrating the process of moderation each year on a sub-set of profile components across the assessment tasks or limiting moderation to two of the tasks;
- including some work within focused tasks or tests that would be relatively highly standardised and thus simple to mark and requiring no moderation after marking;
- focusing the three tasks respectively on mathematical and scientific learning; on literacy and the humanities; and on aesthetics;
- increasing the number of tasks from three to four.

What will the Standard Assessment Tasks be like in the secondary stages?

In the secondary phase, assessment will have to take account of the emergence at 11 of subject emphases and the organisation of the delivery of the curriculum into subject areas. Thus assessment is likely to be very largely subject based and will draw on a wide range of knowledge, skills and understanding particular to the subject. In as far as cross-curricular themes are assessed, however, the SATs at ages 14 and 16 may have to include the aspects of these which are germane to the subject concerned.

It has been suggested that in art, music and physical education, the Government will issue guidelines only and not full programmes of study and attainment targets. In these circumstances, it may be that the assessment requirements at the end of the third and fourth key stages in these subjects will not require the development of SATs.

Where, at the end of the fourth key stage, a foundation subject is taken for GCSE, pupils will not be required to undergo other forms of assessment. Indeed with respect to the core subjects – English, mathematics and science – the Secretary of State expects the majority of pupils to enter GCSE and there may not therefore be SATs in these subjects at the fourth key stage. In other foundation subjects, however, SATs will be an alternative form of assessment for those students who have not followed a full GCSE course.

How will GCSE change to take account of the National Curriculum?

As each core and other foundation subject reaches the fourth key stage, the GCSE syllabuses in the subject concerned will be amended to include the programme of study and attainment targets laid down by Statutory Order.

It is not yet clear what other changes will be required. For instance, it may be that in addition to (or instead of) a GCSE result being reported in terms of a grade, there will also be a report on performance within each profile component and even, perhaps, within each attainment target. The more complex the nature of the report required from GCSE, the more GCSE assessment arangements may have to change to make this possible.

Another change with respect to GCSE may be in terms of the syllabuses available. There will be only limited teaching time remaining for subjects other than those within the National Curriculum and many of the subjects which now feature in the pre-16 curriculum may disappear or be subsumed within other subjects. There may therefore no longer be entries pre-16 for many of the exisiting GCSE syllabuses and such syllabuses are likely gradually to be withdrawn.

On the other hand, there may be demand for GCSE syllabuses which enable the programmes of study and attainment targets in more than one subject to be satisfied. Thus we could see the emergence of Combined Humanities syllabuses which encompass the statutory requirements in geography and history or Combined Arts syllabuses which act similarly in relation to art and music. Modular syllabuses may also be devised to allow flexibility of curriculum delivery within the statutory framework.

What will be the form of teacher assessment?

The TGAT report recommends that teachers' assessments over time and in normal learning contexts should play an important part in the assessment of the National Curriculum. This has been accepted by the Government.

Teachers' own ratings should be derived from a variety of methods of evoking and assessing pupils' responses. As a natural part of teaching, teachers are constantly assessing pupils to determine their progress and to plan the next stage of their learning. Such assessment draws on a wide variety of evidence from many sources over a period of time to arrive at a general picture. However, much of this assessment is not sharply focused, and often it is not recorded, at least not in any consistent or coherent way.

The National Curriculum assessment arrangements will seek to draw on this wealth of assessment which is already taking place. However, it will have to be ensured that all relevant areas of the curriculum are assessed for each pupil and that the results are properly recorded. In other words, systematic assessment procedures will need to be introduced into normal classroom work but without either the teacher being over-burdened or the teaching process being constrained.

How will the teacher assessments be moderated?

Moderation is the process of checking the assessments of individual teachers to bring them into line with national standards. Moderation is necessary since teachers in the main only have experience of the standard of achievement of pupils in their own school or locality. Since school catchment areas differ, such experience is rarely representative of the whole population of pupils throughout the country. Moderation places the assessments of the individual teacher into this national context.

The report of the Task Group on Assessment and Testing surveys the various methods of moderation which are available. It recommends 'that group moderation be an integral part of the national assessment system' and 'that it be used to produce the agreed combination of moderated teachers' ratings and the results of the national tests.'

What is group moderation and how would it work in practice?

In group moderation there would be meetings of teachers to review each other's assessments. In the primary sector, such meetings would probably encompass the whole curriculum whilst at the third and fourth key stages they would be more likely to be subject-specific in nature. Teachers from a group of contiguous schools would meet, bringing with them to the meeting two sets of results for each profile component — their own ratings based on assessment during the course and the results from the nationally prescribed Standard Assessment Tasks. The procedure at the meeting would be such as to align local standards with national standards and then to identify any discrepancies in individual schools.

TGAT argues that a group moderation system ensures accuracy of assessment whilst at the same time contributing to staff development by allowing communication between teachers about curriculum and assessment matters. Such communication not only leads to better practice in schools but also allows formative feedback to the subject groups concerned with the future development of the National Curriculum.

What has been the Government's reaction to the TGAT recommendation on group moderation?

On 7 June 1988, the Secretary of State made a statement in Parliament concerning the TGAT report. The following was the reaction to the proposal for group moderation:

> 'The suggestions . . . on the moderation system appear complicated and costly; whilst the Government recognises that the issues involved are complex, the support systems adopted must be sufficiently simple to enable good progress to be made in introducing the national assessment system. We shall be discussing the issues with the School Examinations and Assessment Council and the National Curriculum Council and also with the local education authorities, the examining groups and other appropriate organisations.'

The way in which teacher assessments will be moderated and aggregated with the results from Standard Assessment Tasks has therefore yet to be determined.

6 Reporting the Results

How will the assessment results be used?

Assessment results will be used in four different ways:

- to plan the next steps in a child's education based on achievement to date;
- to assist the teacher to evaluate and improve his/her teaching;
- to give parents information about the achievement of their own child and an indication of how their child's education is progressing;
- to give parents, schools, LEAs and the Government information about a school which allows the performance of that school to be evaluated.

In fact, the teacher can use assessment results to evaluate his/her own performance or to plan the next stage in a child's education without there being a formal reporting procedure. But there must be a proper reporting framework if information is to be supplied to persons or bodies outside the school.

For these 'external' purposes, the reports will have to take two different forms:

- a detailed report on the assessment results of an individual pupil;
- an aggregated report on the results of all pupils within a school at a given key stage.

What will the report of an individual pupil be like?

We have noted that for the purposes of assessment, a subject is broken down into various tiers:

PROFILE COMPONENTS
ATTAINMENT TARGETS
LEVELS

Each subject has a number of profile components; within each profile component there are several attainment targets; and achievement within each attainment target is measured on a scale of levels from 1 to 10.

The Government wishes the reports to be simple and clear. A report to parents on performance in each attainment target would be unnecessarily detailed and complicated. It is likely therefore that the report to parents will be in terms of achievement within each **profile component** in each core and foundation subject.

Thus for instance in **science** at the **third key stage**, parents will be given reports in terms of the two profile components:

- Exploration of Science;
- Knowledge and Understanding of Science.

For there to be a report on a profile component, some way will have to be found of aggregating the levels which a pupil has achieved in the various attainment targets within that component; and unless that aggregation can itself be expressed in a meaningful way, the report will itself be useless. For instance, to add all the levels within a component together and take an average would convey little useful information about a child's performance.

It is probable that by the mid 1990s, a Record of Achievement will have been introduced for every child of compulsory school age. It may well be that when this has happened, the profile component reports will be incorporated into the record in some way.

Will the reports in all subjects be similar?

It is expected that most core and other foundation subjects will be expressed in terms of profile components and attainment targets. Thus it will be possible to report in the way suggested above.

However, the subject structure and assessment arrangements for art, music and physical education are likely to be less prescriptive. The format of the reports in these subjects could therefore be significantly different.

How confidential will the report on an individual child be?

The assessment results for an individual child will be confidential between teachers, the pupil and his/her parents. It will also be possible to use the information within the school, and to pass it to a receiving school on transfer and, if necessary, to the local authority on a confidential basis.

What will reports within schools be like?

Schools will themselves decide how to aggregate component data in order to undertake internal review and evaluation. Within a class, information in each profile component might be aggregated to identify components where there are particular strengths or weaknesses. Within a department, data might be accumulated at class level to compare the performances of different classes and teachers. In an overall school review, the data might be scrutinised at a subject level.

What form will the public reports take?

There will be no legal requirement for primary schools to publish results at the end of the first key stage although the Government strongly recommends that schools should do so.

At the end of the second, third and fourth key stages, schools will be required to publish aggregated results for the whole school. It is not entirely clear what aggregation means in this context. Probably, at least for assessments at 14 and 16, results will be published for each subject (although it has not yet been determined how aggregation of profile components within a subject will be carried out).

The Task Group on Assessment and Testing recommended that aggregation should **not** take place by finding the average level within a class or school for a particular profile component or subject. Rather, TGAT wished aggregated results to be in the form of **distributions** i.e. the results would show the proportion of pupils reaching each relevant level. Thus for key stage 1, for a particular component or subject, the results might appear in the form:

Level 1: 10% of pupils
Level 2: 75% of pupils
Level 3: 15% of pupils

TGAT was also concerned that schools, when publishing results, should be able to place these in context. It saw two influences which could affect the general level of results positively or negatively.

The first influence concerned the variety of socio-economic factors which affect the pupils' capacity to respond to school work. There is a strong association between social background and educational performance of almost all types. TGAT argued that such factors must be taken into account in judging the national assessment results of a particular school. Otherwise there was a danger:

- that a relatively good performance from a school in a disadvantaged area would appear poor in absolute terms; and
- that a school in an advantaged area which was underperforming might still appear good in absolute terms.

TGAT counselled against adjusting results statistically to take account of these effects. Rather it recommended that:

'any report by a school which includes national assessment results should include a general report for the area, prepared by the local authority, to indicate the nature of the socio-economic and other influences which are known to affect schools. This report should give a general indication of the known effects of such influences on performance.'

The second potential influence on results is the standard of the pupils when they start the relevant key stage. Thus in publishing national assessment results, a school might choose to publish the results of the same pupils at the previous key stage. For instance, a secondary school in publishing results at 14 could refer to the standard of pupils when they started the course at 11 by reference to their national assessment results at that age. It then becomes possible as part of the evaluation of the school to judge the 'value-added'. One school might have done particularly well in bringing on a group of pupils with quite low achievement two or three years earlier. In another school, it might be found that pupils had not progressed very rapidly despite a solid foundation.

7 The Timing of the Introduction
— Primary (Key Stages 1 and 2)

How is the introduction of the National Curriculum to be sequenced?

There are provisions with respect to religious education which came into effect in September 1988, and a general requirement to teach the National Curriculum subjects which is effective from September 1989. These are discussed below.

With respect to detailed attainment targets and programmes of study, however, these come on stream subject by subject and are introduced first in the first year of the relevant key stage. That cohort of pupils then continues through each succeeding year of the key stage and ultimately becomes the first to be assessed according to National Curriculum requirements at the end of the key stage. However, the assessments of that first cohort are not actually reported. It is the results of the **second** cohort which are in fact the first published results.

For example, taking English in the second key stage: the attainment targets and programme of study for English in the second key stage become effective in September 1990. In that academic year they will be taught only to pupils in the first year of that key stage i.e. the 7-8 year olds. In September 1991 that class will become the 8-9 year olds and will continue with the attainment targets and programmes of study (and of course the new 7-8 year old class will also start to be taught according to them). In September 1992 the class will become the 9-10 year olds and in September 1993 the 10-11 year olds. This will be their last year of the second key stage and they will therefore be assessed according to National Curriculum arrangements (on an unreported basis) in summer 1994. By this time all pupils in the second key stage will be being taught English in accordance with the detailed National Curriculum requirements.

This is summarised in Table 4.

TABLE 4: PUPILS IN KEY STAGE 2 BEING TAUGHT ENGLISH IN
ACCORDANCE WITH ATTAINMENT TARGETS AND
PROGRAMME OF STUDY

September 1990	7-8 year olds
September 1991	8-9 and 7-8 year olds
September 1992	9-10, 8-9 and 7-8 year olds
September 1993	10-11, 9-10, 8-9 and 7-8 year olds (i.e. all pupils in key stage 2)

We shall look below on a year-by-year basis at the effect of the
introduction of attainment targets and programmes of study for
the different subjects. However, this information is summarised in
two tables:

■ Table 5 which shows for key stages 1 and 2 the dates of first
  introduction of attainment targets and programmes of study in
  the various subjects;

■ Table 6 which shows on a class-by-class and year-by-year basis
  the subjects which must be taught according to detailed
  National Curriculum requirements.

It will be seen that attainment targets and programmes of study
are to be specified subject by subject with subjects being introduced
on a sequential basis. It must be emphasised, however, that this
does NOT imply that the curriculum has to be taught in a single
subject arrangement. The teacher will have freedom to plan and
deliver his/her teaching programme as seems most appropriate. It
is expected that much teaching and learning will continue to be
cross-curricular and thematic in nature. It will then be for the
teacher to ensure that during the teaching/learning programme the
specified attainment targets and programmes of study are covered.

What are the dates when the National Curriculum will start to be taught in schools?

September 1988

The new arrangements with respect to religious education and
collective worship have already come into effect. Since 29

September 1988, all maintained schools (other than special schools) have been required to provide religious education for all pupils who are registered at the school.

In addition, September 1988 also saw the introduction of the part of the Act which requires that all pupils who attend a maintained school (again, other than special schools) take part in a daily act of collective worship. These requirements were discussed in detail in Chapter 2.

TABLE 5: PROVISIONAL TIMETABLE FOR THE INTRODUCTION OF ATTAINMENT TARGETS AND PROGRAMMES OF STUDY (OR GUIDELINES) IN KEY STAGES 1 AND 2

Date of Introduction	Key Stage 1 Age 5-7	Key Stage 2 Age 7-11
September 1989	English Mathematics Science	
September 1990	Technology	English Mathematics Science Technology
September 1991	Geography* History*	Geography* History*
September 1992	Art* Music* PE*	Art* Music* PE*

*Firm announcements are awaited concerning the precise dates for these subjects

TABLE 6: EFFECT ON A YEAR-GROUP BASIS OF THE INTRODUCTION OF ATTAINMENT TARGETS AND PROGRAMMES OF STUDY IN KEY STAGES 1 AND 2*

(Shading indicates that the year-group must be taught according to the full National Curriculum)

Date	Subject	FIRST KEY STAGE		SECOND KEY STAGE			
		5/6	6/7	7/8	8/9	9/10	10/11
SEPT 1989	ENGLISH	▓					
	MATHS	▓					
	SCIENCE	▓					
SEPT 1990	ENGLISH	▓	▓				
	MATHS	▓	▓				
	SCIENCE	▓	▓				
	TECHNOLOGY	▓					
SEPT 1991	ENGLISH	▓	▓	▓			
	MATHS	▓	▓	▓			
	SCIENCE	▓	▓	▓			
	TECHNOLOGY	▓	▓				
	GEOGRAPHY	▓					
	HISTORY	▓					
SEPTEMBER 1992	ENGLISH	▓	▓	▓	▓		
	MATHS	▓	▓	▓	▓		
	SCIENCE	▓	▓	▓	▓		
	TECHNOLOGY	▓	▓	▓			
	GEOGRAPHY	▓	▓				
	HISTORY	▓	▓				
	ART	▓					
	MUSIC	▓					
	PE	▓					
SEPTEMBER 1993	ENGLISH	▓	▓	▓	▓	▓	
	MATHS	▓	▓	▓	▓	▓	
	SCIENCE	▓	▓	▓	▓	▓	
	TECHNOLOGY	▓	▓	▓	▓		
	GEOGRAPHY	▓	▓	▓			
	HISTORY	▓	▓	▓			
	ART	▓	▓				
	MUSIC	▓	▓				
	PE	▓	▓				

*Note: In art, music and physical education, there are likely to be guidelines rather than attainment targets and programmes of study.
The dates for the introduction of geography, history, art, music and physical education are provisional only and are subject to confirmation.

September 1989 – General requirements

From September 1989, primary schools will be required to teach all the core and other foundation subjects for a reasonable time to all pupils in key stages 1 and 2. That is to say, all pupils in the primary phase will be required to study the three core subjects:

- English;
- mathematics;
- science;

and the other foundation subjects:

- geography;
- history;
- technology;
- music;
- physical education.

Pupils in schools in Wales will also be required to study Welsh from September 1989.

(**Note**: Although a modern foreign language is also a foundation subject, it applies only to pupils 11-16.)

The requirements do not define what is meant by 'a reasonable time'. The intention is that pupils should spend sufficient time in studying each of the core and other foundation subjects to make a worthwhile contribution to the achievement of the overall aim of the curriculum, as described in Section 1 of the Act:

'. . . a balanced and broadly based curriculum which:
  (a) promotes the spiritual, moral, cultural, mental and physical development of pupils at the school and of society; and
  (b) prepares such pupils for the opportunities, responsibilities and experiences of adult life.'

September 1989 – Attainment targets and programmes of study

The first attainment targets and programmes of study are due to be introduced in primary schools in September 1989.

For those pupils entering the first key stage, i.e. those just commencing primary education, the attainment targets and programmes of study will be in:

- English;
- mathematics;
- science.

For the first year of operation only – school year 1989/90 – the attainment targets and programmes of study will only apply to pupils who have reached compulsory school age at the start of the autumn term. They will not apply to pupils who become of compulsory school age during the school year. This is intended to relieve the pressure on primary schools, especially small ones, when considerable demands will be placed on their headteachers and teaching staff. While pupils in this category will not be required by law to follow the attainment targets and programmes of study, the Secretary of State very much hopes that schools will choose to do so, as soon as the pupils are ready. In particular, he expects that schools will, wherever possible, start teaching pupils according to the National Curriculum requirements as they reach compulsory school age and start school in the spring and summer terms of 1989/90. From 1990/1 onwards, this will be a statutory requirement.

Also for the school year 1989/90 only, the attainment targets and programmes of study need not apply to 5-6 year olds who are being taught in classes mostly containing children who are a year older – 6-7 year olds. It is felt that a requirement to teach 5 year olds according to the National Curriculum in a class where the 6 year olds were following a different course would cause difficulties for pupil and teacher. Further transitional arrangements will not be required, as from 1990/1 onwards the 6-7 year old cohort will be required to follow the National Curriculum requirements.

September 1990

First key stage   In September 1990 the cohort of pupils which started studying the National Curriculum in English, mathematics and science the previous September will reach their second year of primary education. The new cohort of pupils entering school in September 1990 (or in the spring or summer terms 1991) will also be taught according to the attainment targets and programmes of study for those three subjects. Thus by September 1990, **all** pupils in the first key stage will be following the attainment targets and programmes of study in English, mathematics and science.

In September 1990, arrangements for the first foundation subject other than the core subjects will be introduced. Attainment targets and programmes of study in **technology** will be introduced for 5 year old pupils starting the first key stage.

When we refer in the above paragraph to 'technology', it must be understood that the term is intended to embrace many aspects of design, as well as technology. Indeed, as we have noted earlier, the working group for this subject is in fact designated 'Design and Technology'. Its interim report makes recommendations about design and IT (Information Technology) as well as for technology.

Second key stage　In September 1990, the first cohort in the second key stage, i.e. the 7-8 year olds, will have to be taught according to the specified attainment targets and programmes of study in the following subjects:

- English;
- mathematics;
- science;
- technology.

September 1991

First key stage　The cohort of pupils which started technology in September 1990 will by this time have reached the second year of key stage 1. Thus **all** pupils in key stage 1 will now be studying English, mathematics, science and technology in accordance with the detailed requirements of the National Curriculum.

In addition, it appears that attainment targets and programmes of study in **geography and history** will be introduced for the first year of key stage 1, although this has yet to be confirmed.

Second key stage　By September 1991, two cohorts of pupils – the 7-8 and the 8-9 year olds – will be studying according to the National Curriculum specification in English, mathematics, science and technology.

In addition, it is likely that attainment targets and programmes of study in **geography and history** will be introduced for the first year of key stage 2, although this has yet to be confirmed.

September 1992

First key stage　All pupils in the first key stage will now be being taught according to the attainment targets and programmes of study in English, mathematics, science, technology, geography and history.

In addition the guidelines in **art, music and physical education** may come into effect for the 5-6 year olds. (This is subject to confirmation.)

Second key stage   By this point, three year groups, the 9-10s, 8-9s and 7-8s, will be following English, mathematics, science and technology; and the 8-9s and 7-8s will be following geography and history.

In addition the guidelines in **art, music and physical education** may come into effect for the 7-8 year olds. Again, this is subject to confirmation.

September 1993

First key stage   By now, the full National Curriculum will have come into effect for all pupils in the first key stage.

Second key stage   All pupils in the second key stage will now be studying English, mathematics, science and technology according to National Curriculum requirements. Geography and history will be being followed by the 9-10s, 8-9s and 7-8s, and art, music and physical education by the 8-9s and 7-8s.

September 1994

All pupils in the second key stage will now be studying English, mathematics, science, technology, geography and history according to the National Curriculum specification and all except the 10-11 year olds will be studying art, music and physical education.

September 1995

All pupils in the first two key stages will be following the full requirements of the National Curriculum.

When will assessment arrangements be introduced?

The answer is very soon indeed! The first Orders for assessment arrangements will be introduced at the same time as those for attainment targets and programmes of study. Although the externally prescribed Standard Assessment Tasks will only take place at the end of a key stage, the teacher assessment will take place throughout the key stage. Assessment by teachers will begin in parallel with the teaching related to attainment targets and programmes of study.

As a result, assessment by teachers will begin in September 1989 for mathematics, science and English in the first key stage.

The national arrangements for formal assessment will bring together the results of teacher assessments and the Standard Assessment Tasks, at the end of the appropriate key stage. This will happen in June 1991 in the first instance. Those pupils who start on attainment targets and programmes of study in mathematics, science and English at the beginning of the infant stage in September 1989 will have completed the first key stage by then.

However, this first cohort of pupils will not have the results of their assessments reported to parents (or, in aggregated form, to local education authorities), as will be the case in later years. The first assessment results to be communicated to parents and other bodies will be those of the second cohort of pupils to be assessed at each key stage. The assessment of pupils in the first cohort at each key stage may therefore be considered to be experimental.

So, those pupils who are 5 years old by the beginning of the autumn term 1989 will be assessed at the age of 7 in 1991, but the results of these assessments need not be communicated to parents or more generally.

It will be different for the next cohort of pupils in the first key stage; those who will be 5 in September 1990. They will reach the age of 7 in 1992, and their assessments will be the first to be reported.

This will be a general principle in the introduction of assessment arrangements; each time attainment targets and programmes of study are introduced at the beginning of a key stage for a particular foundation subject, the first cohort of pupils to begin that key stage will not have their assessments reported. The second, and subsequent, cohorts in that key stage will have the results of their assessments communicated to parents and, in aggregated form, to other bodies.

Thus, when attainment targets and programmes of study in technology are introduced for 5 year olds in September 1990, their assessments in the summer of 1992 will not be reported. Those 5 year olds who begin the first key stage in technology in the autumn term 1991 and who will therefore be formally assessed in June 1993, will have their assessments reported.

An outline timetable for the introduction of reported and unreported assessment in the core and other foundation subjects is given in Table 7.

TABLE 7: PROVISIONAL TIMETABLE FOR THE INTRODUCTION OF ASSESSMENT AT THE END OF KEY STAGES 1 AND 2

END OF STAGE

	Summer 1991	Summer 1992	Summer 1993	Summer 1994	Summer 1995	Summer 1995
KEY STAGE 1	Unreported Assessment in English Mathematics Science	Reported Assessment in English Mathematics Science Unreported Assessment in Technology	Reported Assessment in Technology Unreported Assessment in Geography History	Reported Assessment in Geography History		
KEY STAGE 2				Unreported Assessment in English Mathematics Science Technology	Reported Assessment in English Mathematics Science Technology Unreported Assessment in Geography History	Reported Assessment in Geography History

Note: Art, music and physical education are not included since it is not known whether there will be formal assessment arrangements in these subjects.

8 The Timing of the Introduction
– Secondary (Key Stages 3 and 4)

How is the introduction of the National Curriculum to be sequenced?

There are provisions with respect to religious education which came into effect in September 1988, and a general requirement to teach the National Curriculum subjects which is effective from September 1989. These are discussed below.

With respect to detailed attainment targets and programmes of study, however, these come on stream subject by subject and are introduced first in the first year of the relevant key stage. That cohort of pupils then continues through each succeeding year of the key stage and ultimately becomes the first to be assessed according to National Curriculum requirements at the end of the key stage. However, the assessments of that first cohort are not actually reported. It is the results of the **second** cohort which are in fact the first published results.

For example, taking mathematics in the third key stage: the attainment targets and programme of study for mathematics in the third key stage become effective in September 1989. In that academic year they will be taught only to pupils in the first year of that key stage i.e. the 11-12 year olds. In September 1990 that class will become the 12-13 year olds and will continue with the attainment targets and programmes of study (and of course the new 11-12 year old class will also start to be taught according to them). In September 1991 the class will become the 13-14 year olds. This will be their last year of the third key stage and they will therefore be assessed according to National Curriculum arrangements in summer 1992. By this time all pupils in the third key stage will be being taught mathematics in accordance with the detailed National Curriculum requirements.

This is summarised in Table 8.

TABLE 8: PUPILS IN KEY STAGE 3 BEING TAUGHT MATHEMATICS IN ACCORDANCE WITH ATTAINMENT TARGETS AND PROGRAMME OF STUDY

September 1989	11-12 year olds
September 1990	12-13 and 11-12 year olds
September 1991	13-14, 12-13 and 11-12 year olds (i.e. all pupils in key stage 3)

We shall look below on a year-by-year basis at the effect of the introduction of attainment targets and programmes of study for the different subjects. However, this information is summarised in two tables:

- Table 9 which shows for key stages 3 and 4 the dates of first introduction of attainment targets and programmes of study in the various subjects;
- Table 10 which shows on a class-by-class and year-by-year basis the subjects which must be taught according to detailed National Curriculum requirements.

What are the dates when the National Curriculum will start to be taught in schools?

September 1988

The new arrangements with respect to religious education and collective worship have already come into effect. Since 29 September 1988, all maintained schools (other than special schools) have been required to provide religious education for all pupils who are registered at the school. It should be remembered that this includes pupils who are over the age of compulsory education; sixth form pupils in a secondary school and students attending a sixth form college.

In addition, September 1988 also saw the introduction of the part of the Act which requires that all pupils who attend a maintained school (again, other than special schools) take part in a daily act of collective worship. These requirements were discussed in detail in Chapter 2.

September 1989 – General requirements

From September 1989, secondary schools will be required to teach all the core and other foundation subjects for a reasonable time to all pupils in key stage 3. That is to say, all pupils in that stage will be required to study the three core subjects:

- English;
- mathematics;
- science;

and the other foundation subjects:

- geography;
- history;
- technology;
- a modern foreign language
- music;
- art;
- physical education.

Pupils in schools in Wales will also be required to study Welsh from September 1989.

The requirements do not define what is meant by 'a reasonable time'. The intention is that pupils should spend sufficient time in studying each of the core and other foundation subjects to make a worthwhile contribution to the achievement of the overall aim of the curriculum, as described in Section 1 of the Act:

> '. . . a balanced and broadly based curriculum which:
> (a) promotes the spiritual, moral, cultural, mental and physical development of pupils at the school and of society; and
> (b) prepares such pupils for the opportunities, responsibilities and experiences of adult life.'

The requirement to teach the core and other foundation subjects for a reasonable time will not apply to pupils in the fourth key stage – fourth and fifth year secondary school pupils from September 1989. It is expected that the requirement will be extended to these pupils in the following year – from September 1990.

TABLE 9: PROVISIONAL TIMETABLE FOR THE INTRODUCTION OF ATTAINMENT TARGETS AND PROGRAMMES OF STUDY (OR GUIDELINES) IN KEY STAGES 3 AND 4

Date of Introduction	Key Stage 3 Age 11-14	Key Stage 4 Age 14-16
September 1989	Mathematics Science	
September 1990	English Technology	
September 1991	Geography* History*	
September 1992	Foreign Language* Art* Music* PE*	Mathematics Science English
September 1993		Technology
September 1994		Geography* History*
September 1995		Foreign Language* Art* Music* PE*

*Firm announcements are awaited concerning the precise dates for these subjects

TABLE 10: EFFECT ON A YEAR-GROUP BASIS OF THE INTRODUCTION OF ATTAINMENT TARGETS AND PROGRAMMES OF STUDY IN KEY STAGES 3 AND 4*

(Shading indicates that the year-group must be taught according to the full National Curriculum)

FOURTH KEY STAGE		THIRD KEY STAGE			Subject	Year
15/16	14/15	13/14	12/13	11/12		
				▓	MATHS	SEPT 1989
				▓	SCIENCE	
			▓	▓	MATHS	SEPT 1990
			▓	▓	SCIENCE	
				▓	ENGLISH	
				▓	TECHNOLOGY	
			▓	▓	MATHS	SEPT 1991
			▓	▓	SCIENCE	
			▓	▓	ENGLISH	
			▓	▓	TECHNOLOGY	
				▓	GEOGRAPHY	
				▓	HISTORY	
		▓	▓	▓	MATHS	SEPTEMBER 1992
		▓	▓	▓	SCIENCE	
		▓	▓	▓	ENGLISH	
		▓	▓	▓	TECHNOLOGY	
			▓	▓	GEOGRAPHY	
			▓	▓	HISTORY	
				▓	FOR. LANG.	
				▓	ART	
				▓	MUSIC	
				▓	PE	
▓	▓	▓	▓	▓	MATHS	SEPTEMBER 1993
▓	▓	▓	▓	▓	SCIENCE	
▓	▓	▓	▓	▓	ENGLISH	
	▓	▓	▓	▓	TECHNOLOGY	
		▓	▓	▓	GEOGRAPHY	
		▓	▓	▓	HISTORY	
			▓	▓	FOR. LANG.	
			▓	▓	ART	
			▓	▓	MUSIC	
			▓	▓	PE	

*Note: In art, music and physical education, there are likely to be guidelines rather than attainment targets and programmes of study. The dates for the introduction of geography, history, a modern foriegn language, art, music and physical education are provisional only and are subject to confirmation.

September 1989 – Attainment targets and programmes of study

The first attainment targets and programmes of study are due to be introduced in secondary schools in September 1989.

For those pupils entering the third key stage, i.e. the 11-12 year olds who in general are just commencing secondary education, the attainment targets and programmes of study will be in:

- mathematics;
- science.

September 1990

In September 1990 the cohort of pupils which started studying the National Curriculum in mathematics and science the previous September will start the second year of the third key stage.

A new cohort of 11-12 year old pupils will also be taught according to the attainment targets and programmes of study for those two subjects. In addition, attainment targets and programmes of study in **English and technology** will be introduced for this cohort.

When we refer in the above paragraph to 'technology', it must be understood that the term is intended to embrace many aspects of design, as well as technology. Indeed, as we have noted earlier, the working group for this subject is in fact designated 'Design and Technology'. Its interim report makes recommendations about design and IT (Information Technology) as well as for technology.

September 1991

The cohort of pupils which started mathematics and science in September 1989 will by this time have reached the third year of key stage 3. Thus **all** pupils in key stage 3 will now be studying mathematics and science in accordance with the detailed requirements of the National Curriculum. The 11-12s and 12-13s will also be studying English and technology.

In addition, it appears that attainment targets and programmes of study in **geography and history** will be introduced for the first year of key stage 3, although this has yet to be confirmed.

September 1992

Third key stage   All pupils in the third key stage will now be being taught according to the attainment targets and programmes of study in English, mathematics, science and technology. Two cohorts, the 11-12 and 12-13 year olds will also be studying geography and history.

For the first time, pupils in the first cohort of the third stage may also be required to study **a modern foreign language** in accordance with attainment targets and a programme of study. In addition the guidelines in **art, music and physical education** may come into effect for the 11-12 year olds. The timetables for all these subjects are, however, provisional.

Thus it is probable that all core and foundation subjects will now be being taught in accordance with the specified attainment targets and guidelines to at least one cohort in this third key stage.

Fourth key stage   In September 1992, the first cohort in the fourth key stage, i.e. 14-15 year olds, will have to be taught according to the specified attainment targets and programmes of study in the following subjects:

- English;
- mathematics;
- science.

September 1993

Third key stage   At this time, all pupils in this key stage will probably be studying English, mathematics, science, technology, geography and history and the 11-12s and 12-13s will in addition be following the National Curriculum in a modern foreign language, art, music and physical education.

Fourth key stage   All pupils will be studying English, mathematics and science. In addition, the attainment targets and programme of study in **technology** will be introduced for the first cohort of the fourth key stage.

September 1994

Third key stage   All pupils in the third key stage will now be studying all the core and foundation subjects in accordance with the National Curriculum requirements.

Fourth key stage   By September 1994, **all** pupils in the fourth key stage will be following the attainment targets and programmes of study in English, mathematics, science and technology.

In addition, attainment targets and programmes of study in **geography and history** will probably be introduced for the first year of key stage 4.

September 1995

All pupils will now be following English, mathematics, science, technology, geography and history. The last foundation subjects will now be introduced and the first cohort will be required to follow **a modern foreign language** in accordance with the specified attainment targets and programme of study; and **art, music and physcial education** in accordance with the guidelines.

September 1996

All pupils in compulsory education will now be studying the complete National Curriculum.

When will assessment arrangements be introduced?

The answer is very soon indeed! The first Orders for assessment arrangements will be introduced at the same time as those for attainment targets and programmes of study. Although the externally prescribed Standard Assessment Tasks will only take place at the end of a key stage, the teacher assessment will take place throughout the key stage. Assessment by teachers will begin in parallel with teaching related to attainment targets and programmes of study.

As a result, assessment by teachers will begin in September 1989 for mathematics and science in the third key stage.

The national arrangements for formal assessment will bring together the results of teacher assessments and the Standard Assessment Tasks, at the end of the appropriate key stage. For secondary school pupils, this will happen in June 1992 in the first instance. Those pupils who start on attainment targets and programmes of study in mathematics and science in September 1989 will have completed the third key stage by then and will be formally assessed in these subjects in June 1992.

However, this first cohort of pupils will not have the results of their assessments reported to parents (or, in aggregated form, to local education authorities), as will be the case in later years. The first assessment results to be communicated to parents and other bodies will be those of the second cohort of pupils to be assessed at each key stage. The assessment of pupils in the first cohort at each key stage may therefore be considered to be experimental.

So, those pupils who begin key stage 3 in 1989 will be assessed at age 14 in 1992. But the results of these assessments need not be communicated to parents or more generally.

It will be different for the next cohort of pupils in the third key stage; those who will be 11 in September 1990. They will reach 14 in 1993, and their assessments will be the first to be reported in the secondary sector.

This will be a general principle in the introduction of assessment arangements; each time attainment targets and programmes of study are introduced at the beginning of a key stage for a particular foundation subject, the first cohort of pupils to begin that key stage will not have their assessments reported. The second, and subsequent, cohorts in that key stage will have results of their assessments communicated to parents and, in aggregated form, to other bodies.

Thus, when attainment targets and programmes of study in technology are introduced for 11 year olds in September 1990, their assessments in the summer of 1993 will not be reported. Those 11 year olds who begin the first key stage in technology in the autumn term 1991, and who will therefore be formally assessed in June 1994, will have their assessments reported.

An outline timetable for the introduction of reported and unreported assessment in the core and other foundation subjects is given in Table 11.

TABLE 11: PROVISIONAL TIMETABLE FOR THE INTRODUCTION OF ASSESSMENT AT THE END OF KEY STAGES 3 AND 4

		END OF STAGE				
	Summer 1992	**Summer 1993**	**Summer 1994**	**Summer 1995**	**Summer 1996**	**Summer 1997**
KEY STAGE 3	Unreported Assessment in Mathematics Science	Reported Assessment in Mathematics Science Unreported Assessment in English Technology	Reported Assessment in Technology Unreported Assessment in Geography History	Reported Assessment in Geography History Unreported Assessment in Foreign Language	Reported Assessment in Foreign Language	
KEY STAGE 4			GCSE in Mathematics English Science	GCSE or Reported Assessment in Technology	GCSE or Reported Assessment in Geography History	GCSE or Reported Assessment in Foreign Language

Note: Art, music and physical education are not included since it is not known whether there will be formal assessment arrangements in these subjects.

Will there be a clash between National Curriculum assessment and the GCSE?

There is no requirement in the Education Reform Act for particular subjects to be taken at GCSE level. It is expected, however, that nearly all pupils should take GCSE examinations in the core subjects of English, mathematics and science. It is further expected that many pupils will take four or five further subjects to GCSE level; but not all of these need be foundation subjects.

We might suppose that a particular pupil is starting GCSE courses in English, mathematics, science, French, physical education, religious education and economics. The first five of these subjects are National Curriculum foundation subjects, the last two are not. The remaining five foundation subjects must still form part of the pupil's curriculum in the fourth and fifth years. Attainment targets, programmes of study and assessment arrangements in foundation subjects other than the core will be expected to take into account that some pupils will not take them on to GCSE, but will nevertheless need to continue with them on a worthwhile, if perhaps more limited basis, building on what has been learnt in earlier key stages.

As a result, in a foundation subject other than the core, pupils at the end of the fourth key stage may either sit a GCSE examination or, if they do not take the subject on to this level, receive a reported assessment for the National Curriculum. The pupil described above would need to follow courses and be assessed in art, music, history, geography and technology as well as the seven GCSE subjects!

Assessment at the end of the fourth key stage is likely to require modifications to GCSE National Criteria and the design and production of revised syllabuses by the examining groups. Revised GCSE syllabuses in the core subjects of English, science and mathematics will need to be available in good time for introduction in September 1992. Revised syllabuses in technology will be required for September 1993.

9 Implications for Schools

What are the major implications of the National Curriculum for schools?

The Education Reform Act has major implications for schools and how they operate. This is particularly so in the area of the curriculum and its assessment, where schools will need to consider:

- the **changes** that will be required in their curriculum, organisation, management and use of resources;
- the **information** that they will have to supply to parents, the local education authority and the Government.

What preparations will the Government require?

The introduction of the National Curriculum will require considerable adjustments to the curriculum in many schools. These changes will require corresponding adjustments to the schools' organisation and management and the ways in which resources are used. To help local education authorities to meet the costs of all these changes, the Government is making funds available through Education Support Grants (ESGs) and the Local Education Authority Training Grant Scheme (LEATGS, also known as GRIST), starting in the financial year 1989/90.

In order to qualify for these grants, LEAs will have to base their bids on a systematic review of the curricular, organisational and management changes which the introduction of the National Curriculum will require in each of their schools. To provide LEAs with the necessary information on which to base their bids, every LEA-maintained school − primary, secondary or special − will be asked to produce a **National Curriculum Development Plan**. These plans are intended to help schools and LEAs to establish their priorities for change, target their resources and make any necessary changes to organisation and management structures to meet future requirements most effectively.

Each school's National Curriculum Development Plan will need to take into account the local education authority's curriculum policy and any statements of curriculum aims produced by the school's governing body. It will also need to be compatible with other documents and plans drawn up by the LEA or by the school. While the development plan might form part of a more comprehensive set of documents including schemes of work and the school prospectus, it is primarily intended as a management tool for the LEA and the school.

The plan will need to look forward into the future, while at the same time being manageable and realistic. A timescale of three to five years is likely to be most suitable. This will enable the focus to be on the early years of operation, while allowing known and likely future requirements to be included. Consideration of some of the foundation subjects will need to be provisional in the first instance, until detailed requirements are known. The plans will need updating, on at least an annual basis, to include further National Curriculum requirements as they are developed.

What will be the content of the National Curriculum Development Plan?

Plans should focus on the curriculum as a whole, as well as on corresponding elements of the school's organisation and management structures. In particular, they should:

- give an outline description of the school's **current provision**, in order to provide a baseline of information for further development;
- indicate the **changes** needed to meet the requirements of the National Curriculum;
- give an indication of the school's **priorities** for the changes that are required;
- give an outline **timetable** for the introduction of the changes.

What curricular changes will the school need to consider?

Schools should begin their review of curricular requirements by producing an outline description of the current curriculum and its organisation. This can then be compared with the known statutory requirements and any gaps identified. In addition, necessary changes can be considered. These might include:

- the preparation or revision of schemes of work;
- the development of whole school assessment and reporting policies;

to reflect the statutory requirements.

Schools will need to consider the whole curriculum in order to examine the relationship between the National Curriculum, the statutory requirements for religious education, cross-curricular themes and courses in non-foundation subjects. The school's curricular provision will need to be planned to take into account the basic requirement laid out in the Education Reform Act for a curriculum which:

- is broad, balanced and differentiated;
- promotes the spiritual, moral, cultural, mental and physical development of the pupils at the school and of society;
- prepares pupils for the opportunities, responsibilities and experiences of adult life.

Priorities for change and the corresponding timescale will need to reflect the statutory requirements currently in operation and the Government's proposed timetable for the introduction of the remainder of the National Curriculum. In particular, schools should take into account the requirement to teach pupils, other than those with statements of special educational needs, all foundation subjects for a reasonable time from September 1989 in each of the first three key stages — for the majority of pupils between ages 5 and 14.

In addition to satisfying this general requirement, schools will need to consider the more detailed requirements for attainment targets, programmes of study and associated assessment arrangements as they are progressively introduced. In the first instance this will involve focusing on the introduction in September 1989 of the three core subjects: English, mathematics and science for those entering key stage 3. But schools will also need to consider the adequacy of provision for the other foundation subjects and religious education as well as for non-foundation subjects and cross-curricular themes. Plans for these areas may need revision as the statutory requirements in the other foundation subjects become known.

What about the organisation of the curriculum?

Schools will need to decide on the organisation that will be required to deliver the proposed curriculum. This will involve consideration of:

- the **organisation of teaching groups,** including arrangements for pupils of different ages and different abilities;
- the **amount of integrated and subject-specific teaching** and the balance between them;
- the **provision for statemented children** and others with special educational needs;
- for individual pupils, the **general balance of subjects** within their timetables;
- the **teaching time** which is available during the school day.

In each case, consideration will need to be given to the current organisation of the curriculum and any changes which will be needed to provide the kind of curriculum required by the Education Reform Act. In addition, schools will need to decide on the priorities for such changes and when it is intended to introduce them.

What are the management implications?

There is considerable variation in the degree of control that schools are able to exercise over the resources at their disposal. As **Local Management of Schools** is introduced progressively from April 1990, more schools will have a greater say in decisions relating to resource allocation. Regardless of the amount of delegation currently enjoyed by schools and the timetable over which LMS will be introduced, schools will need to give consideration to the following:

- the current use of resources at their disposal;
- how this resource allocation relates to the planned curriculum and its organisation;
- the changes needed in the use of existing and planned resources;
- the priorities for the changing demand on resources and the timescale for implementing the changes.

Without doubt, the most crucial area for decision-making will be that of staffing the school, both in terms of the number of staff and the necessary balance of expertise. Decisions will need to be made on the optimum use of the staffing resources currently available to the school, including;

- teaching staff;
- non-teaching staff, such as clerical and secretarial support, librarians, technicians, foreign language assistants and classroom ancillaries;
- any additional staff − teaching and non-teaching − for children with special educational needs, both with and without statements.

Particular thought should be given to the need for appointment of new staff to match the new curriculum requirements.

Consideration will also need to be given to the use of in-service training to develop the expertise of existing members of staff.

There will be two sorts of in-service provision; that which will be necessary to prepare all teaching staff for the new National Curriculum requirements and more specific training needed to develop and enhance the expertise of certain staff in particular subjects. For a fuller discussion of the likely provision for in-service training in the National Curriculum see Chapter 10.

Schools will also need to give consideration to the provision and allocation of other resources, including:

- books and other materials;
- equipment;
- teaching spaces;
- information resources such as computer facilities and library provision.

What about pupils with statements of special educational needs?

The general requirements outlined in this chapter also apply to special schools. They should produce National Curriculum Development Plans in 1989, even though the introduction of National Curriculum requirements does not have to apply to statemented children until September 1990. Special schools are, of course, permitted to introduce the National Curriculum requirements to such children, wholly or in part, in September 1989 if they so wish.

Every school, whether special or mainstream, will need to identify the steps it intends to take to ensure that pupils with statements of special educational needs have the maximum access possible to the National Curriculum. Schools will need to consider whether every pupil should study all the National Curriculum foundation subjects. They will also need to examine each subject closely and decide whether to advise the local education authority of any modification or disapplication of the National Curriculum which might result in an amendment to the statement of special educational needs.

Where the National Curriculum requirements have not been modified or disapplied, schools will need to outline any changes in the curriculum, organisation or resource allocation needed to ensure that the requirements can be delivered from September 1990. These changes may need to be amended as the statements are reviewed during 1989/90. All schools, including special schools, will need to update their National Curriculum Development Plans as further details of the requirements become known, including any further particular arrangements for pupils with special educational needs.

What duties concerning information requirements does the Act lay on schools?

Schools will be under a legal obligation to supply and publish certain information about the school curriculum and its assessment. Section 22 of the Education Reform Act enables the Secretary of State to make the necessary regulations; these will be published in due course and are likely to cover the following matters:

■ information to be contained in the school prospectus;
■ information to be provided to parents;
■ information to be provided to the LEA and the Secretary of State.

What information about the National Curriculum must a school provide in its prospectus?

In order that parents choosing a school should know what is on offer to all pupils and age groups, every school will be required to include the following information in its prospectus:

■ information about how to see the LEA's curriculum policy statement and all the relevant documents concerning the National Curriculum;
■ the governing body's statement of its own curricular aims;
■ a statement about the length of lessons, the school session and the school year;
■ a statement about the organisation of the curriculum (including the National Curriculum), the options which are available and the approved external qualifications for which courses are provided;
■ the arrangements made for work experience for older children;
■ information about how to make a complaint and how to gain access to details of the complaints procedure.

The above requirements will probably come into force in September 1989.

What information about the National Curriculum must a school provide for parents?

Schools will of course have to provide a report to parents on the results of their children in the assessments made in the National Curriculum subjects at the end of each key stage. These assessments are discussed in detail in Chapter 6.

There will however be additional information which schools are likely to have to provide or make available to parents as follows:

- at least one copy for inspection by parents of all the relevant Statutory Instruments about the National Curriculum and its assessment, together with associated circulars;
- information about how to see the LEA's curriculum policy statement;
- the governing body's statement of its own curricular aims.

These requirements will probably come into force in September 1989. In addition, the following information requirements will be piloted in 1989/90 for probable introduction in September 1991.

- The provision of a separate piece of paper for each pupil, specific to that pupil, containing the following:

    - a summary of the curriculum plan and objectives for the pupil, explaining any departures from the National Curriculum;
    - a list of any external qualifications for which the pupil is following a course of study.

- What subjects are being studied by the individual pupil, with information about how the National Curriculum programmes of study and the religious education syllabus are being provided and what other subjects and cross-curricular topics are being dealt with;
- The National Curriculum programmes of study and attainment targets for the year ahead;
- How to gain access to schemes of work for each class;
- Details of the next assessments, including external examinations.

LEAs will be asked to consider whether the information which is to be provided to parents should be translated into languages other than English.

_____

What information must a school provide for the LEA?

It is the responsibility of the LEA to monitor and facilitate the provision of the curriculum, particularly the National Curriculum, in its maintained schools. To assist this undertaking, schools will be required to provide LEAs with the following information:

- subjects offered and time spent on them for all age groups;
- the organisation of the curriculum, including cross-curricular themes;
- the length of the school day and the school year;
- the external qualifications and the associated syllabuses for which the school provides courses;
- staff used to deliver the curriculum, showing the use of their time, subject by subject, in relation to their qualifications and relevant INSET experience.

All the above requirements, with the exception of the last, are likely to come into effect in September, 1989.

10 In-Service Training and Other Support

How will the Government support the introduction of the National Curriculum?

The Government will support the introduction of the National Curriculum in a number of ways:

- funding through the **provision of grants**. These are the **Education Support Grants (ESG) and the Local Education Authority Training Grant Scheme** (LEATGS). In broad terms, the ESG programmes provide for general, and particularly non-teaching, support. The LEATGS provides support for the in-service training of local education authority staff, including teachers;
- the provision of a **programme of training** designed by the National Curriculum Council (NCC) and the School Examinations and Assessment Council (SEAC). This will include the development of training materials;
- exceptionally, for 1989 only, **two additional days** on which schools are allowed to close in order to provide their whole staff with training specifically directed to the National Curriculum requirements.

What are Education Support Grants?

The aim of Education Support Grants is to encourage local education authorities to employ a limited amount of expenditure on activities which the Secretary of State decides are of particular importance. They are intended to promote improvements in education provision and to help LEAs to respond to changing needs. The grants are not intended to lead to an increase in overall LEA expenditure. In 1989-90, the Government will support total expenditure of £125.5m through a total grant of £81.5m. In order to qualify for the full grant, LEAs will have to fund the difference between the total expenditure and the grant − £44m.

What Education Support Grants will be available to support the National Curriculum?

Education Support Grants will be available for general support related to:

- the introduction of science, mathematics, technology and English;
- 'English Language in the Curriculum';
- LEA inspection.

Introduction of the core subjects and technology

Existing ESG support for primary science and technology, and for the teaching of mathematics, will need to be redirected by local education authorities towards preparing teachers to deliver the attainment targets, programmes of study and related assessment arrangements which will apply in these subjects from September 1989.

In addition, a grant will be available to support new expenditure of up to £9.5m in 1989-90. This is intended to help schools to introduce as effectively as possible the National Curriculum requirements which apply from September 1989. Further funds are likely to be available in subsequent years − until 1993-4 − for continued support, as the new requirements in relation to the core subjects and technology are progressively introduced.

Subject to satisfactory bids, all LEAs will receive funds to support a range of additional provisions. This is expected to focus on non-teaching support in respect of primary mathematics and science, as the existing ESGs in the teaching of mathematics, and in primary science and technology, will continue to support teachers directly, at least until 1990.

The funds will be allocated on the basis of a formula; half pro rata to the number of pupils in the first and third key stages and half pro rata to the number of primary and secondary schools. The sort of support which LEAs are expected to provide includes the appointment and training of non-teaching staff, appointment and support of advisory teachers and the purchase of books, materials and equipment.

In autumn 1989, LEAs will have to bid for further grants for the four years to 1994. These bids are to be based on a systematic review of schools' requirements, obtained through the preparation by each school of a National Curriculum Development Plan related to the changes in curriculum, organisation and use of resources that will be required.

'English Language in the Curriculum'   Grants of up to £4.8m will be available in 1989-90 for the provision of in-service training to familiarise teachers with the model of the English language described in the Kingman Report. This is intended to prepare all primary teachers and all secondary English teachers for the introduction of attainment targets and programmes of study in English. It is expected that the programme will continue for three years, with total expenditure of £5.6m in 1990-91 and £4.6m in 1991-2.

LEAs, with the exception of ILEA, will form themselves into regional groups of about five to ten LEAs. There will be between 10 and 20 of such consortia. Each consortium will appoint one expert trainer from April 1989 to undertake a centrally prepared training package. From September 1989, each LEA will appoint a primary advisory teacher who will be trained by the expert trainers.

In 1990-91, the expert trainers will train secondary heads of English departments. During the same period, the primary advisory teachers will train one teacher, where possible a language specialist, in each primary school. The final stage will involve these teachers training their colleagues in school.

LEA inspection   Grants will be available for the five years from 1989 to 1994 to support new expenditure on LEA advisory services. The following objectives are to be met:

- the development of a coherent inspection policy for each LEA which will allow it to monitor the quality of education, the implementation of the National Curriculum and the operation of Local Management of Schools (LMS) in terms of educational performance in its schools;
- the recruitment of additional advisers or inspectors where there is inadequate coverage of aspects of the National Curriculum and LMS within an LEA's existing advisory service.

It is intended that the additional advisers or inspectors should advise schools on the progressive introduction of the National Curriculum, and in particular the preparation of development plans. With regard to LMS, it is expected that they will monitor the progress of the pilot schemes and contribute to in-service planning and provision. Once the LEA's statutory scheme of financial delegation is established, the monitoring and evaluation role will be increasingly important.

Priority is expected to be given in 1989-90 to the appointment of additional inspectors in the primary phase, and in those subjects – English, mathematics and science – for which attainment targets and programmes of study will be introduced from September 1989. The amount of expenditure proposed for 1989-90 is £1.9m which will support the appointment of one extra inspector by each LEA other than ILEA. The proposed expenditure of £5.3m in 1990-91 will support the appointment of a second additional inspector in each LEA. Expenditure in the remaining years will be £7.7m in 1991-2, £6.9m in 1992-3 and £3.8m in 1993-4; this will provide for a third extra inspector in half the LEAs in 1991-2, and a fourth in a quarter of authorities in 1992-3.

What is the Local Education Authority Training Grant Scheme?

The Local Education Authority Training Grant Scheme (LEATGS) is designed to support in-service training. Its aims are to:

- promote the professional development of teachers and certain other professional groups;
- promote more systematic and purposeful planning of in-service training;
- encourage more effective management of the teacher force and the other professional groups involved;
- encourage training to meet selected needs which are accorded national priority.

The scheme therefore supports expenditure on types of training identified as national priorities at a higher rate of grant than for expenditure on local priorities.

Which national priority areas will support the introduction of the National Curriculum?

There are ten national priority areas in the 1989-90 Local Education Authority Training Grant Scheme. Of these, two are specifically for National Curriculum training. They are:

- training for the National Curriculum: management and assessment;
- training for the National Curriculum: content.

In addition, existing national priority areas for training in the teaching of mathematics and science will need to be directed as far as possible towards the preparation of teachers for the introduction of attainment targets, programmes of study and associated assessment arrangements in those subjects from September 1989.

Management and assessment   The Secretary of State believes that the establishment of a coherent programme of preparation and training for teachers and local authority advisers and inspectors is an essential component in the effective and controlled introduction of the National Curriculum, including the arrangements for assessment. The National Curriculum Council and the School Examinations and Assessment Council are co-operating on the design of the in-service programme and the production of supporting materials. Until these are completed, LEAs will consider how they can best adapt their existing in-service training programmes to meet the current National Curriculum demands. This national priority area also includes within it training with respect to the needs of the GCSE and the developments of Records of Achievement.

Eligible training comprises training in the management and assessment involved in the introduction of the National Curriculum, and in particular:

- training for **headteachers** and other senior staff to prepare them for managing the introduction and implementation of the National Curriculum, including the preparation of National Curriculum Development Plans;
- training in the **organisation and delivery** of the National Curriculum, the use of **attainment targets**, and the teaching of **cross-curricular themes** given the requirements of the core and other foundation subjects;

- training in the interpretation of **programmes of study** and their conversion into schemes of work;
- training in **assessment and testing** methods and procedures. This may include training in the assessment of GCSE coursework;
- training in the **monitoring and recording** of pupils' progress and achievement and in methods of reporting this information to parents and other agencies;
- each of the above with regard to pupils with **special educational needs**;
- training for **inspectors and advisers** in methods of monitoring, inspecting and reporting on the implementation of the National Curriculum.

Content   The Secretary of State considers that priority should be given within this area to training in the core subjects and technology. This will include training, retraining and updating to address the issue of the shortage of suitably qualified teachers of mathematics, science and technology. The implementation of attainment targets and programmes of study for the core and other foundation subjects will require training in the content of these subjects for both primary and secondary teachers.

Each of the National Curriculum subject working groups has been asked to set out the contribution its subject can make to the teaching of cross-curricular themes and to include them in the formulation of attainment targets and programmes of study. This national priority area therefore includes training in those themes specified in the terms of reference of the various subject working groups, including industry, the economy and the world of work.

Eligible training for teachers, advisers and inspectors comprises training:

- to introduce the programmes of study in the **core subjects and technology**;
- for the **foundation subjects**;
- with regard to the content and approaches to **cross-curricular themes**;
- each of the above as they apply to children with **special educational needs**.

How has the programme of training been devised?

In response to the requests from the Government for initial advice, the National Curriculum Council and the School Examinations and Assessment Council outlined the early stages of a rolling programme of in-service training. It is based on the following principles:

- The National Curriculum Council and the School Examinations and Assessment Council will work together to produce a single coherent rolling programme of training for the National Curriculum and its associated assessment arrangements;
- The primary responsibility for providing in-service training for teachers must lie with the local authorities. LEAs should be encouraged to work together in consortia and to co-operate with institutions of Higher Education;
- HE institutions will be expected to incorporate elements related to the National Curriculum in their initial teacher training courses;
- NCC and SEAC will be responsible for the provision of training materials to support the in-service training programme;
- The training programme will involve an awareness-raising exercise for headteachers, teachers, LEA officers and others;
- The programme will also focus on the introduction of the subject-specific attainment targets and programmes of study and on the development of skills and confidence in the assessment arrangements;
- The National Curriculum involves a new curriculum framework and new assessment arrangements, but not necessarily changes in teaching approaches or learning styles. As a result, the training requirements are not the same as those for the GCSE;
- There should be as little disruption to pupils and schools as possible;
- Evaluation will be built in from the start.

Local authorities' in-service training programmes will largely be funded through the Local Education Authority Training Grant Scheme with additional funding through ESG. Grant support for institutions of Higher Education will have to take account of the need to ear-mark funding for their involvement in in-service training and the need to incorporate National Curriculum materials in their initial training courses.

What are the elements in the proposed rolling programme?

In reply to a Parliamentary question on 4 November 1988, Kenneth Baker announced a programme of early training for teachers and local education authority officers, advisers and inspectors. This training would take place during the calendar year 1989 and would provide the basis for the shape and design of further in-service training provision as proposed by the National Curriculum Council and the School Examinations and Assessment Council. The proposed rolling programme during 1989 includes:

- a series of conferences about the curriculum and assessment proposals to inform and prepare senior education officers in LEAs, higher education and professional associations;
- regional one-day courses in the spring of 1989 to prepare LEA officers, advisers and inspectors;
- one-day courses in the late spring or early summer of 1989 for headteachers, primary subject co-ordinators in English, mathematics and science and heads of science and mathematics in secondary schools;
- two training days during the summer and autumn terms for all teachers. These would take place on school closure days.

What will be the content of the training courses?

LEA officers   These preparatory courses should cover the following:

- the timetable, priorities and scope of the National Curriculum, including management and organisation issues for headteachers and other senior staff;
- priorities for in-service training;
- identification and training of 'lead' trainers;
- School Development Plans;
- using programmes of study to amend existing schemes of work;
- preliminary consideration of whole curriculum and cross-curriculum issues;
- the changing role of governors and their increased responsibilities for the curriculum;
- the outline process for exemption of children with special educational needs;

- first steps to be taken with relation to assessment.

Headteachers, co-ordinators and heads of department
These one-day introductory courses for heads and curriculum
leaders will be adapted from the LEA officers' course above,
but would concentrate on the essentials that schools must
introduce in September 1989. The content will include the
following:

- reassurance about existing competences and skills;
- an outline of future advice, support and training particularly in
  areas where professional expertise is limited, such as primary
  assessment;
- the importance of early familiarisation and awareness of the
  National Curriculum for all staff;
- discussion of strategies for informing and involving parents and
  governors;
- for headteachers, discussion of the DES Information Circular;
- initial consideration of content of mathematics, science and
  primary English requirements;
- the methodology needed to facilitate school-based INSET.

Teachers   These two-day awareness-raising and familiarisation
courses will be based on the training imparted in the courses for
heads and curriculum leaders, and on in-service materials provided
by NCC and SEAC. The content will need to cover:

- the essentials of the courses outlined above;
- adaptation of existing teaching content to the National
  Curriculum requirements contained in attainment targets and
  programmes of study;
- content enrichment where required, especially in primary
  science;
- assessment, monitoring, recording, moderation, information for
  parents;
- cross-curricular and whole curriculum matters.

Materials   The National Curriculum Council is working on the
preparation of materials to support the programme of in-service
training, and it is hoped that these will be made available in good
time for each stage of the training initiative the Council has
proposed. The School Examinations and Assessment Council will
also be contributing appropriate materials, based on the
assessment requirements, to the training programme.

The major thrust of support will be through the provision of distance learning materials. These are likely to comprise broadsheets and INSET activities relating to the core subjects, using video examples of good classroom practice.

Why has the Secretary of State decided to allow schools to close for two days for National Curriculum training?

In his speech to Parliament on 4 November 1988, the Secretary of State defined the major objective of the training to take place before September 1989. This was to increase general awareness of the new arrangements, including the assessment arrangements which would be required. It is intended to provide a basis from which teachers can begin planning for the implementation of these arrangements in the classroom. It is further recognised that once this awareness-raising training has taken place, there will be a need for more specific training for particular subjects and in assessment arrangements.

The Secretary of State recognised that LEAs' plans for in-service training in 1989 were already well advanced, and that, as a result, special arrangements would need to be made. On the recommendation of the National Curriculum Council, endorsed by the School Examinations and Assessment Council, he has agreed that for the calendar year 1989 **only** schools will be allowed to close for two additional days. These days will be focused on whole staff training directed to the new National Curriculum requirements. These additional days may be used for general awareness-raising training which will be needed by all teachers before they begin to work within the new framework in September 1989. Alternatively, they may be used for supplementary training in the autumn term. In any case, the closures will have to take place during the 1989 calendar year.

How will Higher Education be involved?

Institutions of Higher Education may be involved in the in-service training for the National Curriculum in two ways:

- as **providers of initial training** for students preparing to join the teaching profession;

■ as **'lead' trainers** as part of the overall training programme.

Initial training   During the autumn term 1988, there was a series of NCC and HMI conferences designed to raise the awareness of National Curriculum issues among the delegates, who included representatives from Higher Education. In the spring term of 1989, DES and NCC planned to collaborate with Higher Education to ensure that initial training courses in the summer term for all final year and PGCE students included familiarisation and awareness-raising. This would allow LEAs to follow through this training in the students' induction year. The training would involve introduction to programmes of study in English, science, mathematics and technology. Support materials for the training would be provided by the National Curriculum and School Examinations and Assessment Councils. During the autumn term of 1989, Higher Education institutions will need to amend their initial training programmes. Again, support materials will be provided by the Councils.

'Lead' trainers   Higher Education has frequently been involved in the in-service education and training of teachers. It seems likely that this will continue with the introduction of the National Curriculum. The National Curriculum Council envisages representatives of Higher Education being 'lead' trainers and as such having an important role in the training of support staff, heads, curriculum leaders and teachers.

The NCC suggestions for an LEA action plan for in-service training for the National Curriculum are to be found in Table 12.

TABLE 12: NCC SUGGESTIONS FOR LEA ACTION PLAN FOR
IN-SERVICE TRAINING

ELEMENTS			
Audience	**Contents**	**Timing**	**Providers**
Senior LEA staff	Awareness raising INSET planning National Curriculum	Spring 1989 1 day minimum	LEA senior management NCC Training agency
'Lead' trainers from LEA + HE or training agency	As above + training skills	Spring 1989	LEA/HE/ training agency
Support staff: advisory teachers etc.	As above + subject-specific preparation in maths, science, English	Spring/summer 1989 1 day minimum	Lead trainers
Heads: primary, middle secondary (also governors)	National Curriculum Whole school issues Development planning	Spring/summer 1989 1 day minimum	Lead trainers + support staff
Subject co-ordinators and heads of department (maths, science, primary English)	National Curriculum Subject-specific preparation	Spring/summer 1989 1 day minimum	Lead trainers + support staff
Teachers: maths, science (key stages 1 and 3) English (key stage 1)	National Curriculum Subject-specific preparation	2 closure days Summer/autumn 1989	As above + heads, curriculum leaders

11 Summaries of the Documents Published So Far

This chapter gives brief summaries of the documents published so far in relation to the National Curriculum. These include the report of the Task Group on Assessment and Testing and its three supplementary reports, and reports and Orders in English, mathematics, science and design and technology. These four subjects are at different stages in the process which leads to the publication of Statutory Orders.

The Orders for mathematics and science were published in March 1989. There are, consequently, five documents in each case; the interim and final reports of the subject groups, the National Curriculum Council consultation report, the draft Orders and the Orders themselves. In the case of English, there is the subject working group report for ages 5 to 11. For design and technology, there is as yet only the interim report of the subject working group.

Mathematics

The interim report of the Mathematics working group was published on 30 November 1987, and the final report on 30 June 1988. After carrying out a statutory process of consultation on the proposals made by the Secretaries of State, the National Curriculum Council published its consultation report on 30 November 1988. This report was accepted in full by Kenneth Baker. As a result, draft Orders for mathematics were produced and circulated to all organisations who were formally consulted by the National Curriculum Council. The draft Orders, dated 19 December 1988, required those bodies consulted to submit evidence and representations by 3 February 1989. The final statutory Orders were laid before Parliament in March.

Attainment targets

'Mathematics for Ages 5-16', the final report of the mathematics working group, recommended 15 attainment targets. These were grouped into three profile components:

- knowledge, skills and understanding in number, algebra and measures;
- knowledge, skills and understanding in shape and space and handling data;
- practical applications of mathematics.

For assessment and reporting purposes, the working group also recommended that the three components should carry the following weightings;

knowledge, skills and understanding in number, algebra and measures	knowledge, skills and understanding in shape and space and data handling	practical applications of mathematics
30%	30%	40%

In their proposals, published as an introduction to the final report, the Secretaries of State expressed unease about two issues concerned with the three attainment targets in practical applications of mathematics: using mathematics, communication skills and personal qualities:

- the statements of attainment defined by the working group might prove difficult to assess unambiguously, especially in the case of personal qualities;
- for a given level, the statements of attainment were different, depending on the child's age. This, it was felt, would be confusing to parents, teachers and pupils.

Consequently, the Secretaries of State proposed that the attainment targets for practical applications of mathematics should be re-examined, and where possible combined with those for the other two profile components. In addition, they proposed that the statements of attainment should be modified so that they were defined at each of ten distinct levels.

A further area of concern expressed by the Secretaries of State related to the weightings given to the three profile components.

They felt that the weightings suggested by the working group gave too little emphasis to 'the essential foundation of knowledge, skills and understanding which pupils need to tackle practical problems'. As a result, they recommended that much greater weighting should be attached to the other two profile components than to practical applications of mathematics.

In its consultation report, the National Curriculum Council commented on the attention paid to the issue of profile component 3 – practical applications of mathematics. Most of the individuals and bodies consulted had expressed a preference for its retention, albeit in a modified form. In practice, the Council had not been satisfied that the attainment targets could be expressed in ten distinct levels. It seemed better, therefore, to incorporate as much as possible into the other two profile components.

As a result, the National Curriculum Council recommended that the attainment target for personal qualities should be removed, and that the other two attainment targets in practical applications of mathematics – using mathematics and communication skills – should be combined into a new attainment target entitled 'using and applying mathematics'.

This new target is to be included in each of the profile components, and focuses on:

- the pupils' capacity to use and apply the mathematics they are currently engaged in learning to practical tasks;
- the pupils' capacity to use and apply the mathematics with which they are already familiar in tackling theoretical or 'real life' problems.

The addition of the new attainment target in each profile component to the 12 targets recommended in the working group's final report produces the following list of 14 attainment targets, grouped in two profile components:

AT1	Using and applying mathematics:	use number, algebra and measures in practical tasks and real-life problems.
AT2	Number:	understand number and number notation.
AT3	Number:	understand number operations (addition, subtraction, multiplication and division) and make use of appropriate methods of calculation.

AT4	Number	estimate and approximate in number.
AT5	Number/algebra:	recognise and use patterns, relationships and sequences, and make generalisations.
AT6	Algebra:	recognise and use functions, formulae, equations and inequalities.
AT7	Algebra:	use graphical representation of algebraic functions.
AT8	Measures:	estimate and measure quantities and appreciate the approximate nature of measurement.
AT9	Using and applying mathematics	use shape and space and handle data in practical tasks and real-life problems.
AT10	Shape and space:	recognise and use the properties of two-dimensional and three-dimensional shapes.
AT11	Shape and space:	recognise location and use transformations in the study of space.
AT12	Handling data:	collect, process and record data.
AT13	Handling data:	represent and interpret data.
AT14	Handling data:	understand, estimate and calculate probabilities.

These attainment targets, together with their associated statements of attainment, with examples now form part of the Statutory Orders.

The National Curriculum Council recommended that the attainment targets should be grouped into two profile components:

Profile components	Attainment targets	Weighting
1 Knowledge, skills, understanding and use of number, algebra and measures	ATs 1-8	60%
2 Knowledge, skills, understanding and use of shape and space and data-handling	ATs 9-14	40%

Programmes of study

The mathematics working group, in its final report, provided a number of recommendations with regard to programmes of study. These included general guidance on the production of schemes of work, which followed 'the spirit of the Cockcroft Report, and the developments since then relating to new technology'. In addition, the group produced a 'Map of the Mathematics Curriculum' which outlined the main activities which pupils would need to cover in order to make progress within the attainment targets. It was this chart which the Secretaries of State proposed should form the basis for Statutory Orders for mathematics programmes of study.

The National Curriculum Council listed the following guidelines upon which the design and balance of any plan or scheme of work should be based:

- activities should bring together different areas of mathematics;
- the order of activities should be flexible;
- activities should be balanced between tasks which develop knowledge, skills and understanding and those which develop the ability to tackle practical problems;
- activities should be balanced between the applications of mathematics and ideas which are purely mathematical;
- activities should be balanced between those which are short in duration and those which have scope for development over an extended period;
- activities should, where appropriate, use pupils' own interests or questions either as starting-points or as further lines of development;
- activities should, where appropriate, involve both independent and co-operative work;
- tasks should include those which have an exact result or answer and those which have many possible outcomes;
- activities should be balanced between different modes of learning: doing, observing, talking and listening, discussing with teachers and other pupils, reflecting, drafting, reading and writing;
- activities should encourage pupils to use mental arithmetic and pencil-and-paper methods, and to become confident in the use of a range of mathematical tools and new technology.

It is intended that the Council will produce non-statutory guidance on the development of programmes of study and schemes of work based on the recommendations of the mathematics group. These will assist the implementation of the Statutory Orders.

In the Orders themselves, programmes of study are written for each of ten levels. The levels are related to the four key stages as specified in Schedule 2 to the Order:

Key stages	Programmes of study
First key stage	Levels 1 to 3
Second key stage	Levels 2 to 6
Third key stage	Levels 3 to 8
Fourth key stage	Levels 4 to 10

By way of example, the Level 1 programme of study is as follows:

Using and applying mathematics	Using materials for a practical task. Talking about own work and asking questions. Making predictions based on experience.
Number	Counting, reading and writing numbers to at least 10. Understanding conservation of number. Using addition and subtraction with numbers no greater than 10. Reasonable estimation of a number of objects up to 10.
Algebra	Copying, continuing and devising repeating patterns.
Measures	Comparing objects without measuring; using appropriate language.
Shape and space	Sorting and classifying 3-D shapes. Building 3-D solid shapes and drawing 2-D shapes and talking about them. Giving and understanding instructions for movement along a line. Appreciating spatial properties through moving shapes.
Handling data	Selecting criteria for sorting a set of objects, and applying them consistently. Recording with objects or drawing. Creating simple mapping diagrams showing relationships and interpreting them. Recognising possible outcomes of random events.

Science

The timetable for the production of Statutory Orders for attainment targets and programmes of study in science was identical to that for mathematics; the science working group published its interim report on 30 November 1987 and its final report on 30 June 1988; the National Curriculum Council published its consultation report at the end of November 1988; Draft Orders were published in the middle of December 1988 and the Statutory Orders were laid before Parliament in March 1989.

Attainment targets

In its final report 'Science for ages 5 to 16', the science working group recommended 22 attainment targets for pupils aged 11 to 16 of which 17 were to apply to pupils aged 7 to 11.

These attainment targets were grouped into four profile components:

- knowledge and understanding;
- exploration and investigation;
- communication;
- science in action.

The last of these — science in action — was not to apply to pupils in the first two key stages.

The working group recommended that the four profile components should carry the following weightings at each of the reporting ages:

Profile Component	Reporting Age %			
	7	11	14	16
Knowledge and understanding	35	35	40	40
Exploration and investigation	50	50	30	25
Communication	15	15	15	15
Science in action	—	—	15	20

The Secretaries of State, in their proposals at the beginning of the report, expressed concern about the group's recommendations:

- There were too many profile components – three for pupils aged 5 to 11 and four for pupils aged 11 to 16;
- Some of the statements of attainment in the six attainment targets for exploration and investigation, communication and science in action lacked the necessary precision, especially with regard to personal qualities;
- The targets in exploration and investigation, communication and science in action were defined with relation to pupils' ages and therefore achievement of a particular level might mean different things for pupils at different ages. This was felt to be confusing to all those involved – parents, pupils and employers;
- The weightings for the four profile components at the different reporting ages were felt to give too little emphasis to knowledge and understanding.

As a result of these concerns, the Secretaries of State proposed that the attainment targets in exploration and investigation, communication and science in action should be re-examined and , where possible, included in the profile component for knowledge and understanding. The number of profile components, they recommended, should be reduced to two, or three at the most, and there should be a significantly higher relative weighting given to knowledge and understanding at each reporting age. Finally, they proposed that the group's recommendations for attainment targets should be modified so that each should be defined in terms of ten distinct levels, irrespective of age.

The working group had recommended that at least one-sixth of curriculum time in secondary schools should be devoted to science. The Secretaries of State expressed doubt as to the realism of this for all pupils. They therefore proposed that consideration be given to the production of a balanced science programme which some pupils might cover in about $12^{1}/_{2}$ per cent of time in years 4 and 5. This would lead to a single GCSE certificate for such pupils.

The National Curriculum Council, in its consultation report, supported the view expressed by many respondents that the full programme of study should be followed by all pupils. Nevertheless as required by the Secretaries of State, the Council indicated the key elements needed in a balanced science course for the minority of pupils who would follow such a course.

The consultation process also indicated widespread concern about proposals to increase the relative weighting for knowledge and understanding; indeed, many wanted the weighting for the exploration and investigation component at ages 7 and 11 to be increased. Similarly, there was considerable opposition to the proposal that the attainment targets in exploration and investigation, communication and science in action should be included with those for knowledge and understanding.

Following the consultation exercise, the National Curriculum Council recommended that there should be two profile components − exploration of science and knowledge and understanding of science. Communication and science in everyday life are highlighted in each programme of study. The new profile component − exploration of science − comprises one attainment target. Knowledge and understanding of science comprises 16 attainment targets of which 13 apply to key stages 1 and 2.

All the attainment targets which were in the working group's report have been amended, some significantly. The 17 attainment targets recommended by the National Curriculum Council, and since included in Statutory Orders, are as follows:

AT1   Exploration of science;

AT2   The variety of life;

AT3   Processes of life;

AT4   Genetics and evolution;

AT5   Human influences on the earth;

AT6   Types and uses of material;

AT7   Making new materials;

AT8   Explaining how materials behave;

AT9   Earth and atmosphere;

AT10 Forces;

AT11 Electricity and magnetism;

AT12 Electronics and the scientific aspects of Information Technology;

AT13 Energy;

AT14 Sound and music;

AT15 Using light and electromagnetic radiation;

AT16 The Earth in space;

AT17 The nature of science.

Three of the attainment targets — making new materials, explaining how materials behave and the nature of science — do not apply to pupils in primary schools.

The proposed model for those pupils who are to follow a single award science course in key stage 4 contains the following ten attainment targets:

AT1   Exploration of science;

AT3   Processes of life;

AT4   Genetics and evolution;

AT6   Types and uses of material;

AT8   Explaining how materials behave;

AT9   Earth and atmosphere;

AT10 Forces;

AT11 Electricity and magnetism;

AT13 Energy;

AT14 Sound and music.

It is proposed that the weightings allocated to the two profile components should be as given below;

Key stage	1	2	3	4
Exploration of science	50	45	35	30
Knowledge and understanding of science	50	55	65	70

(all figures %)

As an example of the statements of attainment, the following are those for level 4 of AT1 Exploration of science. Pupils should:

- suggest ideas which lead to investigations;
- plan and safely carry out an investigation where the plan indicates that the relevant variables have been identified and others controlled;
- formulate a testable hypothesis;
- construct 'fair tests';
- select and use a range of measuring instruments, as appropriate, to quantify observations of physical quantities, such as volume and temperature;

- record results by the construction of simple tables, bar charts, pie charts, line graphs, as appropriate;
- draw conclusions from experimental results;
- interpret written instructions and diagrammatic representations;
- describe investigations in the form of ordered prose, using a limited technical vocabulary.

Programmes of study

The Orders provide for programmes of study for each of the key stages 1 to 3 and for double award (Model A) and single award (Model B) science courses in key stage 4.

Programme of study	Attainment targets	Levels
Key stage 1	1 to 6, 9 to 16	1 to 3
Key stage 2	1 to 17	2 to 6
Key stage 3	1 to 17	3 to 8
Key stage 4 (Model A)	1 to 17	4 to 10
Key stage 4 (Model B)	1, 3, 4, 6, 8 to 11, 13, 14	4 to 10

By way of example, the programme of study for level 3 contains the following section relevant to exploration of science. 'Pupils should be encouraged to develop their investigative skills and their understanding of science through systematic experimentation and investigations which:

- are set within the everyday experience of pupils and in wider contexts, which require the deployment of previously encountered concepts and their investigative skills to solve practical problems;
- develop and use an increasingly systematic and safe approach;
- require that pupils plan and carry through investigations in which they may have to vary more than one key variable and where the variable to be measured can be treated continuously;
- require increasingly precise quantitative approaches to measurement of key variables;
- require pupils to make strategic decisions about the number, range and accuracy of measurements, and select and use the appropriate apparatus and instruments;

- encourage systematic recording using methods appropriate to the data and the purpose of the activity;
- encourage the interpretation and evaluation of collected data against the demands of the problem, using mathematical relationships, where appropriate;
- encourage the searching for patterns in data and the ability to make simple predictions based on findings;
- encourage the use of technical vocabulary when reporting findings and conclusions.'

Technology

In addition to its work in science, the working group also gave consideration to attainment targets and programmes of study for technology from 5 to 11. Although their recommendations will not be part of Statutory Orders, it is expected that they will inform the thinking of the design and technology working group.

The working group recommended four attainment targets in technology:

- Technology in context;
- Designing and making;
- Using ideas of force and energy;
- Communicating technology.

The group also recommended the following weightings for these attainment targets;

	7 %	11 %
Technology in context	10	10
Designing and making	60	60
Using ideas of force and energy	10	10
Communicating technology	20	20

English

The English working group was established in April 1988, and produced its first report 'English for ages 5 to 11' on 30 September 1988. This dealt with the National Curriculum requirements for English in the first two key stages. The final report, dealing with the requirements for the third and fourth key stages, is to be produced in May 1989.

Attainment targets

The working group recommended six attainment targets for English for pupils from 5 to 11. One target is proposed for speaking and listening, two for reading and three for writing. Each target encompasses the knowledge, skills and understanding relevant to its particular area.

The six attainment targets are:

- Speaking and listening: pupils should demonstrate their understanding of the spoken word and the capacity to express themselves effectively in a variety of speaking and listening activities, matching style and response to audience and purpose;
- Reading I: the development of the ability to read, understand and respond to all types of writing;
- Reading II: the development of reading and information-retrieval strategies for the purpose of study;
- Writing I: a growing ability to construct and convey meaning in written language;
- Writing II: spelling;
- Writing III: handwriting.

Each attainment target is defined for levels 1 to 5.

The statements of attainment for 'speaking and listening' are as follows:

Level	Description
1	Speak freely, and listen, one-to-one to a peer group member.
	Respond to simple classroom instructions given by a teacher.
2	In a range of activities (including problem-solving), speak freely, and listen, to a small group of peers.
	Listen attentively, and respond, to stories and poetry.
	Speak freely to the teacher, listen and make verbal and non-verbal responses as appropriate.
	Respond to an increasing range and complexity of classroom instructions.

3   Present real or imaginary events in a connected
         narrative to a small group of peers, speaking freely and
         audibly.
         Convey accurately a simple message.
         Give and receive simple instructions and respond
         appropriately.
         Listen attentively for increased periods of time and
         respond as appropriate.

4   Describe an event or experience to a group of peers,
         clearly, audibly and in detail.
         Give and receive precise instructions and follow them.
         Ask relevant questions with increasing confidence.
         Offer a reasoned explanation of how a task has been
         done or a problem has been solved.
         Take part effectively in a small group discussion and
         respond to others in the group.
         Make confident use of the telephone.
         Speak freely and audibly to a class.
         Speak freely and audibly to the adults encountered in
         school.

5   Speak freely and audibly to a larger audience of peers
         and adults.
         Discuss and debate constructively, advocating and
         justifying a particular point of view.
         Contribute effectively to a small group discussion which
         aims to reach agreement on a given assignment.

In their proposals, the Secretaries of State expressed the view that
the statements of attainment would benefit from examples to
demonstrate more precisely differentiation between levels. They
might also be made more specific to provide an adequate basis for
assessment, and the first attainment target in writing should give
more emphasis to grammatical structure.

The group recommended that there should be equal weighting for
the three profile components of speaking and listening, reading
and writing. The Secretaries of State agreed with this view for the
first key stage, but proposed a higher weighting for the reading
and writing profile components at key stage two.

Programmes of study
The report recommended programmes of study in each of the
profile components – speaking and listening, reading and writing.

For speaking and listening, for example, it is suggested that the range of activities should include:

For pupils aged 5 to 7:

- casual talk;
- response to visual and aural stimuli;
- collaborative and exploratory play;
- imaginative play and improvised drama;
- listening to well-chosen and well-read stories, rhymes, poems, plays and other writing, including the writing of other children;
- listening to and telling unscripted stories;
- sharing experiences (gained in and out of school) with the teacher, other pupils and parents;
- asking and answering questions;
- giving and receiving simple explanations and information;
- giving and receiving simple instructions, with opportunities for appropriate response.

For pupils aged 8 to 11:

- casual talk;
- response to visual and aural stimuli;
- imaginative play and improvised drama;
- listening to well-chosen and well-read stories, rhymes, poems, plays and other writing, including the writing of other children;
- listening to and telling unscripted stories;
- working with and devising simple drama scripts;
- sharing experiences (gained in and out of school) with a wide range of audiences;
- asking and answering questions;
- interviewing;
- expressing opinions;
- arguing a point of view;
- giving and receiving explanations and information;
- giving and receiving instructions, with opportunities for appropriate response;
- informal discussion with the teacher (e.g. of a piece of work) or with other pupils;
- collaborative learning and problem solving;
- discussion of an assignment, where a specific outcome is required (e.g. planning a school outing; predicting the end of a story; 'cloze' work on a poem);
- simple summary.

Design and Technology

The design and technology working group was set up on 29 April 1988 to advise on attainment targets, programmes of study and assessment arrangements for design and technology. It was also asked to advise on attainment targets and programmes of study for information technology.

Originally, the group's terms of reference covered only technology for the third and fourth key stages and design and information technology for the first and second key stages. In July 1988, the group's remit was extended to include technology in key stages 1 and 2, taking into account the work already carried out in this area by the science working group. The working group submitted its interim report on 9 November 1988; the final report is to be received in May 1989.

Attainment targets

The working group constructed the following five attainment targets with the possibility of increasing this number slightly at a later stage:

AT1   Explore and investigate contexts for design and technological activities: through exploration and investigation of a range of contexts (personal, social, environmental, business, industrial) pupils should be able to identify and state clearly needs and opportunities for design and technological activities;

AT2   Formulate proposals and choose a design for development: pupils should be able to explore, develop and combine design and technological proposals, and use their judgements, based on various criteria (economic, technical, aesthetic, ergonomic, environmental, social) to choose an appropriate design for further development;

AT3   Develop the design and plan for the making of an artefact or system: pupils should be able to develop their chosen design by refining and adding detail, and to produce a plan for making the required artefact or system by identifying tasks and sub-tasks, and ways of undertaking them, and by making judgements of what is realistic, appropriate and achievable;

AT4   Make artefacts or systems: working to a scheme derived from their previously developed design, pupils should be able to identify, manage and use appropriate resources, including both knowledge and processes, in order to make an artefact or system;

AT5   Appraise the processes, outcomes and effects of design and technological activities: pupils shoud be able to produce a critical appraisal of the processes, outcomes and effects of their own design and technological activity, as well as the outcomes and effects of the design and technological activities of others, both historic and present day. With respect to their own activity, they should be able to use their appraisal to propose and justify modifications to the processes they have used and to the outcomes realised.

The working group formulated these attainment targets in terms of practical capabilities rather than knowledge or skills. The group saw the distinctive quality of design and technology as the ability of pupils to use their knowledge; the knowledge being a means to an end rather than an end in itself.

The group proposed to group the five attainment targets into a single profile component called 'Design and Technological Capability'. They reserved the right to modify this position in the light of their further work.

The working group suggested that the core of knowledge and understanding required in design and technology could be organised in four areas:

- media for design and technology activities: materials, energy and information;
- influences on design and technology practice: range and potential of available tools and equipment, mathematical and aesthetic principles and of business practice and economics;
- characteristics of design and technology products: systems, structures and mechanisms;
- applications and effects of design and technology activity: relationship between scientific and technological advance and the social and economic impact of technological change, both in history and in the contempory world.

The report identified the following skills in design and technology:

- exploring and investigating;

- imaging and speculating;
- organising and planning;
- making;
- communicating and presenting;
- appraising.

Programmes of study

The interim report provided the following extract from the programmes of study relating to AT4 – Making as an illustration of the likely style and format of the final programmes of study:

KEY STAGE 2

Pupils should be taught to make artefacts and systems which they have designed, these terms to be interpreted broadly to include examples as diverse as a climbing frame, a model bridge, a schedule for a school visit, a stage set for a play. The work should be in relation to design intentions which pupils have already formulated and in the context of familiar situations (such as the home, the school, and the local community) and, as appropriate, situations from their own imagination (a desert island, a dance production, a spaceship). Pupils should be taught to work as both individuals and as members of a team engaged in a making task and to acquire and use skills of making, involving a range of tools, equipment and materials, both natural and man-made. Not all construction involves tools, however, and equipment and materials here are intended to include construction kits as well as manufactured components such as switches, batteries, quick release devices, and software.

(i)   Pupils should be introduced to and taught about equipment and hand tools (for example scissors, hand drills, scales, spreadsheets). They should be taught to make informed choices of tools and equipment appropriate to the task in hand (for example glue guns for cardboard model-making, needle and thread for fabricating soft toys) and to the materials to be worked (over a range as diverse as flour, wood, clay, data). Pupils should be taught varied procedures (including measuring, shaping, mixing, joining) and the necessary knowledge and understanding of tools and equipment and their safe and correct use.

(ii) From a range of given everyday materials, pupils should be taught to make informed choices appropriate to the task in hand. They should be taught skills of estimating the requirements of materials and other resources needed for their task (for example, How long will it take? Is the material wide enough? Have we got enough?).

(iii)   Through practice, pupils should be taught about recommended procedures for making and assembling (for example how to load a computer program, how to use adhesives effectively).

(iv)   Pupils should be trained to make judgements about the degree of accuracy which is realistic for the task in hand.

(v)   Pupils should be encouraged through their making activities to develop positive personal qualities such as perseverance, self-reliance, enterprise and ability to collaborate.

Information Technology

The working group's terms of reference required a focus for the development of computer and IT awareness involving attainment targets and programmes of study related to IT and basic computer skills and awareness of the uses of advanced technology. The interim report made the following points:

- Development of IT capability is essential for every pupil; all curricular areas provide appropriate contexts for the use of IT;
- IT forms an essential part of many artefacts and systems;
- Pupils will develop an awareness of the broader principles of IT particularly in design and technology;
- A framework for assessment of pupils' IT capability across the curriculum is required. In its further work, the group will consider the number and nature of attainment targets for general IT capability;
- Progression in IT comes through the increasing demands of the contexts involved;
- The programmes of study for general IT capability must be based on realistic, worthwhile and varied contexts;
- In addition to general IT capability, there is a need to assess IT capability as an integral part of design and technological ability. The final report will provide statements of attainment relating to IT capability at each of the ten levels in the design and technology attainment targets.

Task Group on Assessment and Testing

The Secretary of State set up the Task Group on Assessment and Testing under the chairmanship of Professor Paul Black in July 1987.

Terms of Reference

Its terms of reference were 'to advise on the practical considerations which should govern all assessment including testing at age (approximately) 7, 11, 14, and 16, within a national curriculum; including:

- the marking scale or scales and kinds of assessment to be used;
- the need to differentiate so that the assessment can promote learning across a range of abilities;
- the relative roles of informative and of diagnostic assessment;
- the uses to which the results of assessment should be put;
- the moderation requirements needed to secure credibility for assessments; and
- the publication and other services needed to support the system,

with a view to securing assessment and testing arrangements which are simple to administer, understandable by all in and outside the education service, cost-effective, and supportive of learning in schools.'

The group was further asked to take into account the need to avoid additional calls on teachers' and pupils' time and to advise on the possible staged introduction of assessment arrangements.

The Report – purposes and principles

In its report, submitted to Kenneth Baker on 24 December 1987, TGAT made a number of recommendations.
It listed 18 purposes and principles:

- the basis of assessment should be formative, with diagnostic indications. At 16, it should incorporate summative functions;
- all assessment information about an individual should be confidential;
- results should be aggregated across schools or classes for summative and evaluative purposes;
- assessment of attitudes should not be prescribed;
- pupil results in a subject should be presented as an attainment profile;

- each subject should report a small number of profile components. One or more components should have more general application across the curriculum;
- the national tests – standard assessment tasks – should allow flexibility of form and use;
- assessment tasks should be regularly reviewed for evidence of race or gender bias;
- attainment targets should be exemplified using specimen tasks;
- a mixture of assessment instruments should be used;
- teachers' ratings of pupil performance should be fundamental to the system;
- subject working groups should consider the need for confidence in the assessment when grouping attainment targets into profile components;
- teachers' ratings should be moderated;
- assessment should be based on a combination of moderated teachers' ratings and standard assessment tasks;
- group moderation should be an integral part of the system;
- an item bank of assessment tasks should be available for teachers to use;
- final reports on pupils should be the responsibility of the teacher, supported by standard assessment tasks;
- schools should report the distribution of pupils' marks.

The Report – The assessment system in practice

TGAT produced the following recommendations concerning 'the assessment system in practice':

- the ages for assessment should be 7, 11, 14 and 16, with assessment taking place towards the end of the school year in which each cohort reaches the appropriate age;
- each of the subject working groups should produce a sequence of levels in each of its profile components, related to broad criteria for progression. There should be ten levels of performance if the profile component covers the whole age range from 5 to 16;
- levels 1 to 3 should be used for assessment at age 7;
- there should be only one formal reference point between National Curriculum assessment and GCSE, in the first instance; the boundary between level 6 and level 7 should correspond to the grade F/G boundary for GCSE;
- the subject working groups should adopt current practices for determining the GCSE grades at A/B, C/D, mid E and F/G as a

starting point to develop the top four levels in their profile components;

- GCSE should be retained in its present form, until the national assessment system at earlier ages is under way;

- assessment and reporting should be at the same ages for all pupils, and differentiation should be based on progression through the sequence of ten levels;

- support and training should be provided to help teachers relate their own assessments to those required for the National Curriculum;

- a review should be undertaken of the materials available to schools for diagnostic purposes;

- a working group should be established to co-ordinate the assessment proposals of the various subject working groups at the primary stages. The group should be informed by a comprehensive view of the primary curriculum and the need to avoid overburdening teachers;

- assessment results for individual pupils should be confidential, to be discussed between pupils, teachers and parents and to be transmitted only in confidence. The assessment results for the whole class and whole school should be available to parents;

- the only form in which an individual school's assessment results should be published is as part of a broader report by the school of its work as a whole;

- any report of an individual school's results on the national assessments should be accompanied by a general report for the area, produced by the local education authority, setting out the nature of socio-economic and other factors which are known to affect school performance;

- there should be no requirement to publish the results of national assessments at age 7. For pupils at age 11, aggregated assessment results should be published as part of the school's report;

- for pupils at ages 14 and 16, the national assessment results, aggregated at school level, should be published as part of each school's report;

- for 7 year old pupils, the standard assessment tasks should comprise a choice of three prescribed tasks for each child. Each task should provide opportunities for the systematic assessment of the full range of profile components appropriate at age 7;

- for 11 year old pupils, the tests should include three or four standard tasks covering a range of profile components, possibly supplemented by a number of more narrowly focused tests;

- Records of Achievement should be used as a vehicle for recording achievement within the national assessment system;
- changes will eventually be required in GCSE and other criteria as a result of developments in the National Curriculum;
- wherever pupils with special educational needs are capable of attempting the national tests, they should be encouraged to do so. They too need attainable targets to encourage development and promote self-esteem;
- a special unit within a selected test development agency should be dedicated to the production of appropriate test materials and to the devising of sufficiently wide-ranging and sensitive testing and assessment procedures to respond to the needs of children with special educational needs.

The Report – implementation

On 'implementation', the Task Group on Assessment and Testing made the following five recommendations:

- each subject working group should decide on a small number – usually four – of profile components in relation to which each individual pupil's performance will be assessed and reported. For each profile component, a criterion-referenced set of levels of attainment should be defined, to span the whole age range for which the component is appropriate;
- for each profile component, subject working groups should specify the nature of the national tests – standard assessment tasks – which should be developed. In addition, they should specify the help and advice which teachers should be given in relation to their internal assessments;
- the procedure by which performance levels in profile components are to be aggregated into a subject performance level should be specified. Uniform ways of describing profile components and the levels of attainment within each should be specified in language which is helpful to pupils, parents, teachers, employers and other users;
- subject working groups should give advice about the degree of novelty of assessment that they envisage, so that the construction of such assessments and the provision of appropriate in-service support for teachers can be appraised;
- the assessment system should be phased in over time. This will

allow the preparation and trial of new assessment methods, teacher preparation and extensive experience for pupils of the new curriculum. This period should be at least five years from the dissemination of attainment targets.

Three supplementary reports

TGAT produced three supplementary reports on 25 March 1988.

THE FIRST SUPPLEMENTARY REPORT

The first of these followed the consideration by the group of the responses to its main report. These indicated very positive reactions to the group's proposals from those within the profession and those outside, particularly from parents and parent governors. Nevertheless, the group felt that it needed to explain more fully the implications of some of their proposals, and the first supplementary report attempted to do this.

The aspects covered in this report included:

- attainment targets and teachers' assessments;
- group moderation;
- aggregation of data;
- GCSE links;
- reporting and publication;
- records of achievement;
- security and confidence in results;
- evaluation and review;
- implications for teaching and learning;
- essential features of the system.

In its report, the group reaffirmed the need for a balance between standardised tests (both written and otherwise) and other forms of assessment. It also stressed its view that the use of externally-prescribed tests combined with teachers' own assessments, together with effective moderation procedures, offered the best means of securing standards, enhancing professional skills and improving learning.

THE SECOND SUPPLEMENTARY REPORT

The second supplementary report recorded the outcome of discussions with subject specialists on the application of the proposed assessment framework to individual subjects. As a result, the group suggested that:

- close liaison will be needed between working groups for different foundation subjects. This would secure consistency in the definition of profile components and also ensure that common elements are suitably reflected in each subject, avoiding omission or duplication;
- subject working groups in fields such as the arts should pay particular attention to the balance of assessments. This is because such subjects find it more difficult to assess strands of performance in isolation;
- working groups may need to give priority to developing descriptions of progression, covering the primary phase;
- the groups should clarify their thinking on attainment targets and profile components, especially in the primary phase, by first examining existing assessment and testing items;
- the groups should advise on the circumstances in which different levels of aggregation of results may be appropriate;
- the groups should suggest how in-service training needs in their subjects might be met.

THE THIRD SUPPLEMENTARY REPORT

The third supplementary report presented the group's conclusions about the implementation, administration and support of the assessment system.

The report set out the general criteria which the organisational structure should meet, and the purposes and functions of each body in the system. It recommends a structure involving a regional tier between the national agencies and the moderating groups of up to 20 schools. The regional tier would consist of up to a dozen consortia in English, formed by partnerships of local education authorities and GCSE examining groups. They would be responsible for the co-ordination of assessment procedures, moderation, monitoring and evaluation, curriculum development and in-service training in their regions. The report also sets out arrangements for developing, trialling and supplying assessment instruments to schools.

The report stresses that in-service training and, in the longer term, initial teacher training will be essential. It proposes an awareness-raising programme for headteachers in 1988-9, and programmes of training for primary and secondary teachers to prepare them for continuous assessment, administering standard assessment tasks and moderation from 1989-90 onwards. The model of delivery, it proposes, should be a 'cascade' process, similar to that used for GCSE training.

In a case study, the report indicates how a typical local education authority could redeploy resources currently used for in-service training for other purposes in support of the National Curriculum and assessment. It found that the amount required for this represented only a small proportion of current total in-service provision.

The report does not attempt to estimate the financial costs of its proposals. These would depend on the nature and sophistication of the assessment instruments and the degree of novelty in the curriculum. The main point it makes is that the bulk of the costs of the support and training programme and resource requirements will be as a result of the National Curriculum itself rather than the associated assessment framework. TGAT noted that the Government had made provision for the National Curriculum and assessment in its public expenditure plan for April 1989 onwards.

The Secretary of State's response

In an announcement to Parliament on 7 June 1988, the Secretary of State announced the publication of the group's supplementary advice. He noted that the recommendations of TGAT had been well received and announced the following main principles which the Government had decided to adopt:

- attainment targets to establish what children should normally be expected to know, understand and be able to do at the ages of 7, 11, 14 and 16;
- attainment targets to be grouped, to make the assessment and reporting of pupils' performance at 7, 11, 14 and 16 manageable;
- attainment targets to involve ten levels of attainment;
- assessment by a combination of external tests and teacher assessments. At 16, GCSE to be the main assessment;
- assessment results to be used both formatively and summatively;
- detailed assessment results of individual pupils to be given in full to parents. These reports to parents are to be simple and clear. Individuals' results should not be published, but aggregated results at the ages of 11, 14 and 16 should be, so that 'the wider public can make informed judgements about attainment in a school or LEA'. There should be no legal

requirement for schools to make public such results for 7 year
olds, although the Government will strongly recommend that
schools should do so;
- In order to safeguard standards, teachers' assessments of their
  pupils' attainments should be compared with the results of the
  national tests and with the judgements of other teachers.

The Secretary of State commented about the large amount of work
which he considered needed to be done on the detail of
cost-effective arrangements needed to support the assessment
system. In particular, he said that the moderation system proposed
in TGAT's third supplementary report appeared 'complicated and
costly'.

Glossary of Terms

Aggregation is the process by which the results of different assessments are brought together to produce an overall result. (For instance, levels within attainment targets could be **aggregated** to produce a report on a profile component.)

Assessment refers to all the procedures that contribute to the appraisal of a pupil to produce information about the pupil's qualities or achievements.

Attainment targets are the knowledge, skills and understanding which pupils are expected to have at given points in their education.

Basic curriculum consists of the National Curriculum together with religious education.

Core subjects in terms of the National Curriculum are English, mathematics and science. (Note: In Wales, Welsh is also a core subject for Welsh-speaking schools.)

Coursework is work undertaken by a pupil as part of the normal teaching/learning process and which is then assessed for the purposes of an external report or certificate.

Cross-curricular describes an approach which shows the relationship and interaction between separate subjects by seeking commonality and similarities between them.

Diagnostic assessment is assessment directed towards the identification in detail of the learning difficulties of a pupil in order that appropriate remedial help may be offered to that pupil.

Differentiation is the process of matching teaching, learning and assessment to the ability of the individual pupil so that the pupil may be stretched to the full extent of his/her capability and is given opportunities to demonstrate fully what he/she knows, understands and can do.

Education Reform Act is a parliamentary Act passed in 1988 and covering a number of educational provisions including the National Curriculum.

ESG stands for Education Support Grant, a means by which the Government encourages local education authorities to deploy a limited amount of expenditure on activities which the Secretary of State decides are of particular importance. Education Support Grants are intended to promote improvements in educational provisions.

Examining is one means of assessing. It usually takes place in controlled conditions using predetermined questions or tasks (in, for instance, the form of a written question paper).

Formative assessment is assessment which is undertaken as part of the teaching/learning process in order to reinforce what has been done well, to identify and assist with those elements which have been less successful, and to help plan the next stage of learning.

Foundation subjects are the ten subjects listed in the National Curriculum. Three of these are the core subjects – English, mathematics and science – and the other seven foundation subjects are history, geography, technology, music, art, physical education and a modern foreign language, although the modern language applies only to pupils in the third and fourth key stages. (**Note**: In Wales, Welsh is also a foundation subject.)

GCSE is the General Certificate of Secondary Education, an examination which is taken by the majority of pupils at the end of their compulsory education (16+).

Grant Maintained Schools are schools within the state sector which withdraw from the control of the local education authority and become directly responsible to the Department of Education and Science. The process is known as 'opting out'.

GRIST is Grant Related In-Service Training, now known as LEATGS (qv). Until 1986, any in-service training activity which was approved by the DES qualified for Government funding under a 'pool' arrangement. Since that date, each LEA has been given a total expenditure for in-service training on which the Government is prepared to contribute a fixed percentage known as the grant.

Group moderation is a moderation process, undertaken usually by a number of teachers from contiguous schools, who meet to standardise each other's teacher ratings so that they conform to national standards.

INSET is In-Service Training for Teachers i.e. methods of promoting the ongoing professional development of teachers and extending their knowledge and skill base.

Item bank is a comprehensive collection of assessment questions or tasks which can be drawn upon and used by defined users e.g. teachers.

Key stages are the periods into which the years of compulsory schooling are divided for the purposes of teaching and assessing the National Curriculum. There are four key stages:

Stage One   – ages 5-7 (i.e. the cohorts 5-6 & 6-7)
Stage Two   – ages 7-11 (i.e. the cohorts 7-8, 8-9, 9-10 & 10-11)
Stage Three – ages 11-14 (i.e. the cohorts 11-12, 12-13, & 13-14)
Stage Four – ages 14-16 (i.e. the cohorts 14-15 & 15-16)

LEATGS is the Local Education Authority Training Grant Scheme, previously known as GRIST (qv). It is a Government grant designed to support in-service training. Grant is payable at a higher level for types of training identified as national priorities.

Levels of attainment constitute the scale on which achievement of the attainment targets is measured. There are ten levels covering the full period of compulsory education.

Local Management of Schools (LMS) is the delegation of the management of a school to its local managers – usually the headteacher and the governing body. This was originally known as Local Financial Management (LFM), but it was later recognised that the management tasks to be delegated, whilst having financial aspects, were more wide-ranging than merely the management of the budget.

Moderation is the process of standardising assessments (often teacher ratings) to align them with national standards.

Modular approach is an approach whereby discrete units of curriculum are taught and assessed separately but form part of, or build into, a coherent whole.

National Curriculum is the compulsory curriculum laid down by the Government for all pupils in state schools during the period of compulsory schooling (ages 5-16).

NCC is the National Curriculum Council, a body established under the Education Reform Act to keep under review, and to advise the Secretary of State on, matters concerning the curriculum in maintained schools.

National Curriculum Development Plan is a planning document which each school will be asked to produce by its local education authority. In order to qualify for Government grants to support the introduction of the National Curriculum, LEAs will be expected to carry out a survey in each of its schools on the changes that will be required. This survey will be carried out through the production, by each school, of a National Curriculum Development Plan.

Objectives are statements in terms of knowledge, skills and qualities of desired educational outcomes. Assessment objectives are the particular educational objectives which it is intended to assess in a given test or examination.

Opting out See Grant Maintained Schools.

Oral assessment is the assessment of a pupil's ability (a) to understand the spoken word and (b) to communicate by means of the spoken word.

Order See Statutory Order.

Practical assessment is the assessment of skills of a practical nature which may, according to the subject under consideration, include skills such as artistic, dramatic, experimental, craft, design, physical and motor.

Profile component is a set of attainment targets grouped together for reporting purposes.

Programmes of study are the matters, skills and processes which must be taught to pupils to enable the attainment targets in the various subjects to be met.

Project is a task, often used for assessment purposes, which is open ended in nature and which requires some degree of planning and research by the pupil.

Record of achievement is a document which is drawn up over the whole, or the latter part, of a pupil's school career and which contains evidence of that pupil's achievement and personal qualities.

SACRE is a Standing Advisory Council on Religious Education. It is a body which, in accordance with the Education Reform Act, each LEA must establish to advise on religious education and to determine where the legislative provisions for broadly Christian education and worship need not apply.

SATs are Standard Assessment Tasks. These are tasks which will be externally set and which pupils will take at the end of a key stage. Their purpose is to measure (in conjunction with teacher ratings) the achievement of pupils on the National Curriculum attainment targets.

SEAC is the School Examinations and Assessment Council, a body established under the Education Reform Act to keep under review, and advise the Secretary of State on, all aspects of examinations and assessment.

Secretary of State is the title used in this book to denote the Secretary of State for Education and Science. It should be noted that he usually acts in conjunction with the Secretary of State for Wales with respect to the implementation of legislation in Wales.

Statement of attainment is a description of what a pupil will need to have achieved in order to be placed on a particular level within a give attainment target.

Statutory Order is a parliamentary device whereby certain powers given to ministers in legislation can be put into effect. Statutory Orders require the approval of parliament before they come into effect.

Subject Working Group is an advisory group appointed by the Secretary of State to work out the details of the National Curriculum in a given subject.

Summative assessment records the achievement of a pupil at the end of a given stage in his/her education, that assessment then often being used for the purposes of external report or certification.

Teacher assessment is the assessment by teachers of work undertaken by pupils during the teaching/learning process, that assessment then often contributing to an external report or certificate.

Teachers' ratings are the judgements which teachers make on the coursework of pupils, these judgements usually being expressed in terms of a mark or scale point.

Testing is a particular form of assessment. It usually implies a closely prescribed task undertaken in formal conditions.

TGAT is the Task Group on Assessment and Testing established by the Secretary of State to advise him on structures and systems for assessing the National Curriculum.

TVEI stands for the Technical and Vocational Education Initiative. It began on a pilot basis in September 1983, seeking to make the curriculum more practical and relevant to adult and working life. Through an extension phase, it is now gradually being spread to all schools in the country.

Work experience is an activity undertaken by pupils as part of their education. They spend a short time as an 'employee' in a place of work in order to experience the environment and discipline of employment.